NO LONGER
PROPERTY OF PPLD

D0382508

This Book Belongs to

Book 13

Content and Artwork by
Gooseberry Patch Company

LEISURE ARTS

Editor-in-Chief: Susan White Sullivan
Craft Publications Director: Cheryl Johnson
Special Projects Director: Susan Frantz Wiles
Senior Prepress Director: Mark Hawkins
Art Publications Director: Rhonda Shelby

EDITORIAL STAFF

Technical Writer: Mary Sullivan Hutcheson
Contributing Technical Writer: Laura Siar Bertram
Technical Associates: Frances Huddleston, Lisa Lancaster and Jean Lewis
Foods Editor: Jane Kenner Prather
Editorial Writer: Susan McManus Johnson
Designers: Kim Hamblin, Anne Pulliam Stocks, Lori Wenger and Becky Werle
Art Category Manager: Lora Puls
Lead Graphic Artist: Dayle Carozza
Graphic Artists: Jacob Casleton and Becca Snider
Imaging Technician: Stephanie Johnson
Prepress Technician: Janie Marie Wright
Photography Manager: Katherine Laughlin
Contributing Photographers: Mark Mathews and Ken West
Contributing Photostylist: Christy Myers
Publishing Systems Administrator: Becky Riddle
Mac Information Technology Specialist: Robert Young

BUSINESS STAFF

President and Chief Executive Officer: Rick Barton
Vice President and Chief Operations Officer: Tom Siebenmorgen
Vice President of Sales: Mike Behar
Director of Finance and Administration: Laticia Mull Dittrich
National Sales Director: Martha Adams
Creative Services: Chaska Lucas
Information Technology Director: Hermine Linz
Controller: Francis Caple
Vice President, Operations: Jim Dittrich
Retail Customer Service Manager: Stan Raynor
Print Production Manager: Fred F. Pruss

OXMOOR HOUSE

VP, Publishing Director: Jim Childs
Editorial Director: Susan Payne Dobbs
Brand Manager: Victoria Alfonso
Senior Editor: Rebecca Brennan
Managing Editor: Laurie S. Herr
Editor: Ashley T. Strickland
Project Editor: Diane Rose
Designer: Allison Leigh Sperando
Director, Test Kitchens: Elizabeth Tyler Austin
Assistant Directors, Test Kitchens: Julie Christopher and Julie Gunter
Test Kitchens Professionals: Wendy Ball, Allison E. Cox, Victoria E. Cox, Margaret Monroe Dickey, Callie Nash, Kathleen Royal Phillips, Catherine Crowell Steele, Alyson Moreland Haynes and Leah Van Deren
Photography Director: Jim Bathie
Senior Photo Stylist: Kay E. Clarke
Associate Photo Stylist: Katherine Eckert Coyne
Assistant Photo Stylist: Mary Louise Menendez
Production Manager: Tamara Nall Wilder

CONTRIBUTORS:

Copy Editor: Rhonda Richards
Proofreader: Catherine Fowler
Photo Stylists: Missy Neville Crawford and Mindi Shapiro

Copyright © 2011 by Gooseberry Patch, 2500 Farmers Dr., #110, Columbus, Ohio 43235, www.gooseberrypatch.com (illustrations, recipes and crafts). Copyright © 2011 by Time Home Entertainment Inc., 135 West 50th Street, New York, New York 10020, www.oxmoorhouse.com (layout, photography, crafts and recipes). All rights reserved. This publication is protected under federal copyright laws. Reproduction of this publication is prohibited unless specifically authorized. This includes, but is not limited to, any form of reproduction or distribution on or through the Internet, including posting, scanning or e-mail transmission. We have made every effort to ensure that these recipes and instructions are accurate and complete. We cannot, however, be responsible for human error, typographical mistakes or variations in individual work. Made in the United States of America.

Hardcover ISSN: 2154-4263
Softcover ISSN: 2154-4263

Hardcover ISBN-10: 0-8487-3427-0
Softcover ISBN-10: 0-8487-3428-9

Hardcover ISBN-13: 978-0-8487-3427-5
Softcover ISBN-13: 978-0-8487-3428-2

10 9 8 7 6 5 4 3 2 1

Mary Elizabeth ★ Holly ★ Kate ★ Spot

Christmas

Book 13

Christmas

Gooseberry Patch

Wishing all our family & friends
the best of the holiday season!

Our Story

Back in 1984, we were next-door neighbors raising our families in the little town of Delaware, Ohio. Two moms with small children, we were looking for a way to do what we loved and stay home with the kids too. We had always shared a love of home cooking and making memories with family & friends and so, after many a conversation over the backyard fence, Gooseberry Patch was born.

We put together our first catalog at our kitchen tables, enlisting the help of our loved ones wherever we could. From that very first mailing, we found an immediate connection with many of our customers and it wasn't long before we began receiving letters, photos and recipes from these new friends. In 1992, we put together our very first cookbook, compiled from hundreds of these recipes and, the rest, as they say, is history.

Hard to believe it's been over 25 years since those kitchen-table days! From that original little Gooseberry Patch family, we've grown to include an amazing group of creative folks who love cooking, decorating and creating as much as we do. Today, we're best known for our homestyle, family-friendly cookbooks, now recognized as national bestsellers.

One thing's for sure, we couldn't have done it without our friends all across the country. Each year, we're honored to turn thousands of your recipes into our collectible cookbooks. Our hope is that each book captures the stories and heart of all of you who have shared with us. Whether you've been with us since the beginning or are just discovering us, welcome to the Gooseberry Patch family!

Find us here too!

Join our **Circle of Friends** and discover free recipes & crafts, plus giveaways & more! Visit our website or blog to join and be sure to follow us on Facebook & Twitter too.

www.gooseberrypatch.com

Join our Circle of Friends

YouTube

Find us on Facebook

Read Our Blog

Follow us on twitter

Follow us on Scribd.

Sleigh Bells Ring 8
Make spirits bright with cheery outdoor décor.

Glad Tidings 14
So many beautiful ways to say "Merry Christmas!"

Woodland Gathering 22
Capture the magic of a forest-themed holiday.

Christmas Fun and Games 30
Children will adore the kid-friendly tree and handmade toys.

'Tis the Season to Sew 36
A jolly collection of projects in fabric and thread.

Inspirations 42
Dozens of ideas for greetings, gifts and more!

Handmade Gifts 54
One-of-a-kind creations for your family & friends.

Sweet and Savory Gifts of the Season.. 66
Treats to share, from your kitchen to theirs!

Holiday Open House.................................78
You're invited! Great finger foods for a fun gathering.

Christmas Dinner Classics.....................84
Serve up the most memorable flavors of the past.

Blue Ribbon Cakes 92
A half-dozen of the most indulgent cakes you'll ever bake.

The Yummy Comfort of Casseroles.......98
Everyone's favorite winter foods! So hearty and warm!

Take Five!...104
Just five to seven ingredients are all it takes!

Sensational Citrus!...............................108
Delicious recipes using ingredients from the fruit bowl.

Project Instructions.................114

General Instructions 137

Patterns................................141

Project Index 158

Recipe Index 159

Credits 160

Why not spend a little time on the porch this Christmas? Wrapped in a warm Sweater Throw, you'll stay toasty as you enjoy these wintry outdoor decorations. A small sleigh filled with evergreen trees gets extra cheer from Cardinal Ornaments and Bell Mini-Banner Ornaments. Sleigh bells ring on a Door Basket, painted banner and bell strap. With these jolly projects all around, it's easy to imagine yourself on an old-fashioned sleigh ride...even if there isn't a snowflake in sight!

Sleigh with Trees instructions are on page 114.

Sleigh with Trees

9

Tree Sweater Pillow

- two 22"x22" squares of red knit fabric cut from sweaters
- 11"x11" square of green knit fabric cut from a sweater
- green fabric scrap
- brown felt scrap
- red embroidery floss
- 12 assorted red buttons
- red vintage earring
- polyester fiberfill

1. Stabilize the red knit squares by zigzagging around the edges, using a medium stitch length and width.

2. Enlarge the patterns (page 148) to 200%. Use the circle pattern to cut 12 fabric circles and the trunk pattern to cut a felt trunk. Pin the tree pattern to the green knit fabric and stitch along the pattern edge to stabilize the knit fabric. Cut out the tree ³/4" beyond the stitched line.

3. Turning under along the stitched line as you work, hand sew the tree to a red knit square. Work *Running Stitches* (page 139) with red floss to attach the trunk below the tree. Use red floss to sew the fabric circles, buttons and earring on the tree.

4. Matching the right sides and raw edges and using a ¹/2" seam allowance, zigzag the red sweater pieces together, leaving an opening for turning. Turn right side out, stuff with fiberfill and hand sew the opening closed.

Sweater Throw
Lamp Post Banner

Instructions are on page 114.

Tree Sweater Pillow

Lamp Post Banner

**Cardinal Ornament
Bell Mini-Banner Ornament**

Everyone will love to see Cardinal Ornaments resting in a tree! Jingle bells add color to the Bell Mini-Banner Ornaments. The Sleigh Bell Strap and Door Basket greet visitors with more fun sights of the season…red ribbon and shiny jingle bells!

Cardinal Ornament

- lightweight aluminum flashing
- utility scissors
- gloves to protect hands when working with flashing
- scrap block of wood
- hammer and small nail
- red spray paint
- black and brown acrylic paints and paint brush
- 2½" flat clothespin
- E-6000® adhesive

1. Enlarge the patterns (page 150) to 200%. Draw around the patterns on the flashing. Wearing gloves, cut out the pieces with the utility scissors.
2. On the wrong side of the paper patterns, draw over the wing, tail and eye with a pencil. Place the patterns, right side up, on the flashing wing, body and tail pieces and draw over the detail lines, transferring them to the flashing. Place the flashing pieces on the wood block; use the hammer and nail to punch the eye and the wing and tail detail lines.
3. Working in a well-ventilated area, spray the front and back of each flashing piece red. Paint the face black. Paint the clothespin brown.
4. Glue the wing and tail pieces to the body. Glue the clothespin to the cardinal back.

Bell Mini-Banner Ornament
Sleigh Bell Strap

Instructions are on page 115.

Door Basket

Place florist's foam in a hanging basket and arrange greenery and pinecones in the foam. (If using fresh greenery, line the basket with a plastic bag and moisten the foam before placing it in the basket.)

To add the bow and bells, wrap florist's wire around a multi-loop bow and each bell; then, insert the wires in the foam.

Sleigh Bell Strap

Door Basket

13

Christmas is coming! Spread the word with vintage-look Printing Block Ornaments made from craft foam and wood scraps. The printing blocks are more than decorations, because they're also used to stamp happy phrases on the Printed Tree Skirt, Cozy Thoughts Pillows, Good Cheer Garland and more! Make your holidays jolly with everyday items, such as jar lids that frame a traced snowman or sled. When they're filled with small mementos, plastic wine glasses and glass containers become "Bell Jar" Ornaments and Jar Mini-scapes. Place these festive projects throughout your home to share the glad tidings of the season!

Jar Lid Ornaments
instructions are on page 116.

Jar Lid Ornament

"Bell Jar" Ornament

"Bell Jar" Ornaments

- 5-oz. 2-piece plastic wine glasses
- craft knife or awl
- ornament cap and loop (removed from a purchased ornament)
- ribbon
- super-jumbo bottle cap (available at scrapbook stores) or jar lid
- mementos and other items to encase in ornament
- craft glue
- mica flakes

1. Use the craft knife or awl to make a small hole in the stem of the wine glass piece (discard the base piece). Attach the ornament cap to the glass by inserting the wire loop through the hole. Knot a ribbon length through the wire loop.

2. Place the mementos on the bottle cap or jar lid, gluing as necessary. We enclosed a mini bottle-brush tree and added a little "JOY" banner created with cork stickers and embroidery floss; marked the date with alphabet and number stamps, surrounding them with printed paper tinsel, mini ornaments, and colorful postage stamps; combined red and green postage stamps, a mini clothespin, and a seasonal label for a festive look; and arranged a sentiment rubber stamp with a beribboned key.

3. Glue the wine glass to the bottle cap or jar lid. Run a thin bead of glue around the wine glass rim and sprinkle mica flakes into the wet glue.

Family & friends will be amazed to see all the festive little things on display in the "Bell Jar" Ornaments. You don't have to be an artist to make the merry Jar Lid Ornaments, because the snowman and sled are simply traced onto a circle of acetate. Burlap fabric makes a truly charming Printed Tree Skirt when it's stamped with "Glad Tidings" and trimmed with ordinary upholstery webbing, buttons and rickrack.

Sweater Throw

The happy colors of the Sweater Throw will almost keep you warm all by themselves! The throw and Tree Sweater Pillow are quick to sew using pieces of gently worn sweaters. Share your Christmas spirit with the neighbors by displaying a bell-trimmed Lamp Post Banner.

Printed Tree Skirt

- 48" square of burlap
- string and thumbtack
- water-soluble fabric marker
- craft foam
- wood scraps
- craft glue
- solvent-based permanent ink pad, such as StazOn®
- 8 yards 3½"w upholstery webbing
- embroidery floss
- 4 yards super jumbo rickrack
- three ⅞" dia. red buttons

1. For the skirt, follow *Making a Fabric Circle* (page 137) and use a 23½" string measurement to mark the outer cutting line on the burlap square. Remove the tack and use a 1" string measurement to mark the inner cutting line.

2. Cut through all burlap layers along the drawn lines. Unfold the circle. Cut a back opening from the outer edge to the center opening. Clipping as necessary, press all raw edges ½" to the wrong side twice and hem.

(continued on page 115)

Jar Lid Ornament

Instructions are on page 116.

Jar Lid Ornament

Why not make extra-large Printing Block Ornaments and let them spell out your favorite place to be at Christmas? In fact, printing blocks in all sizes are fun for stamping Cozy Thoughts Pillows and merry gift tags, like the ones on the Mail Box Card Holder and gift packages.

Mail Box Card Holder & Wrappings

For the mailbox, hand sew rickrack to an upholstery webbing length. Secure the webbing around the mailbox. Dress up the card holder with a ribbon and paper tinsel bow, a stamped tag and some jute twine. A button and a bit more rickrack are the final touch for the bow and tag. Brown kraft paper, simple ribbon or twill tape and button-decorated tags combine to wrap the gifts.

Printing Block Ornaments

Once you've stamped the tree skirt and made the garland (page 21), staple ribbon to the wood block stamps for tree ornaments or place the HOME letters on the staircase. To add to the vintage look, *drybrush* (page 138) on some additional paint or smear on some additional ink.

Cozy Thoughts Pillows

Cozy Thoughts Pillows

Home

- two 19" squares of fabric
- craft foam
- wood scraps
- craft glue
- solvent-based permanent ink pad, such as StazOn®
- polyester fiberfill

1. Follow *Making and Using Wood Letter Stamps* (pages 137-138) to make stamps for "HOME." (Our letters are 7"h.) Use stamps and permanent ink to stamp letters in the center of 1 fabric square.
2. Matching the right sides and raw edges and using a ¹/₂" seam allowance, sew the fabric squares together, leaving an opening for turning. Clip the corners, turn the pillow right side out and press. Stuff with fiberfill and sew the opening closed.

Celebrate

- two 19"x13" rectangles of fabric
- craft foam
- wood scraps
- craft glue
- solvent-based permanent ink pad, such as StazOn®
- polyester fiberfill

1. Follow *Making and Using Wood Letter Stamps* (pages 137-138) to make stamp for "Celebrate." (Our word is 14"x8".) Use stamp and permanent ink to stamp word in the center of 1 fabric rectangle.
2. Matching the right sides and raw edges and using a ¹/₂" seam allowance, sew the fabric rectangles together, leaving an opening for turning. Clip the corners, turn the pillow right side out and press. Stuff with fiberfill and sew the opening closed.

Mail Box Card Holder & Wrappings

19

Jar Mini-scapes

Any glass container can easily become a miniature Christmas vignette, so why not invite the older kids to assemble Jar Mini-scapes? The charming landscape on the Framed Pen & Ink Scene doesn't require drawing skills, just the ability to trace a pattern! If anyone asks, you can tell them you made the Good Cheer Garland yourself, including the stamps for the cheerful phrase.

Jar Mini-scapes
Capture a moment in time with these miniature vignettes.

Glue an old-time snowman ornament to the lid of a refrigerator jar. Dot the inside of the jar with craft glue and sprinkle with glitter for a snowy effect. Sprinkle mica flakes at the base of the snowman and glue the lid to the jar. Glue printed paper tinsel around the jar.

A sweet little reindeer is glued in a jar with a dusting of mica-flake snow at his feet. Tie a rickrack length around the jar and add a seasonal message cut from printed paper tinsel.

Nestle a bottle-brush tree in a tin gelatin mold and decorate with assorted buttons, printed paper garland and red *Running Stitched* (page 139) rickrack. Top off the tree with a vintage brooch.

Next, glue the mold into the lid of a large jar. Scatter mica flakes and buttons in the lid. Adhere dimensional snowflake stickers to the inside of the jar. Place the jar over the tree and tighten the lid.

Framed Pen & Ink Scene

- 8"x10" picture frame with glass
- India ink and quill
- toothpick
- fabric for background (we used a heavy linen)
- red embroidery floss
- alphabet stamps and solvent ink pad, such as StazOn®
- craft glue
- mica flakes
- spray adhesive

1. Trace the pattern (page 147) onto the glass with the India ink and quill. Set aside to dry. Lines can be "cleaned up" by gently scraping the dry ink away with a toothpick.

(continued on page 116)

Good Cheer Garland
Instructions are on page 116.

Framed Pen & Ink Scene

Good Cheer Garland

Woodland Gathering

There's something magical about a wintry evening in the woods! This cozy gathering features an easy-to-make Acorn & Pinecone Centerpiece. The napkins and the corners of the tablecloth are embroidered with the woodsy theme, while simple snowflakes add a wintry touch to Window Dressing Garlands and Wrapped Packages. It's an oh-so-sweet setting where your family & friends can share the happiest night of the year!

Evergreen Spray Tablecloth instructions are on page 26.

Evergreen Spray Tablecloth

Acorn & Pinecone Centerpiece

For a cozy arrangement, tuck greenery, Felt Pinecones and Felted Wool Acorns in a simple wooden bowl. Add a few glass ornaments for color.

Felt Pinecone

- 4" or 5" papier-mâché egg
- felt
- craft glue

1. Enlarge the patterns (page 145) to 158%. Cut the scales and stem from felt.
2. Glue a small felt circle to the narrow end of the egg. Fold the stem in half and glue together. Glue the stem to the wide end of the egg.
3. Wrap 1 small scale around the narrow end of the egg, gluing as necessary. Continue adding scales, placing the large scale lengths in the center, the small scale lengths at the stem end, and the medium scales in between. Clip the felt straight edges as necessary to fit the egg. When you reach the stem, cut the individual scales apart and glue them around the stem.

Felted Wool Acorn

- plastic basin
- liquid dishwashing detergent (without scents or dyes)
- wool roving
- foam ball or egg (we used $2\frac{1}{2}$" dia. balls and $3\frac{13}{16}$" long eggs)
- $\frac{8}{32}$" dia. cord – $1\frac{1}{2}$ yards for a ball acorn **or** $2\frac{1}{4}$ yards for an egg acorn
- medium rickrack – 4 yards for a ball acorn **or** $4\frac{5}{8}$ yards for an egg acorn
- fabric glue

(continued on page 117)

Mistletoe Tea Towel

Instructions are on page 117.

Would you believe that the Felt Pinecones and Felted Wool Acorns start off as papier-mâché or foam shapes? Gather them into a bowl for an Acorn & Pinecone Centerpiece. Celebrating one of the fun traditions of the season, the Mistletoe Tea Towel is easy to embroider and highlight with felt "berries." The pretty edging is quick to sew using ribbon and rickrack.

Mistletoe Tea Towel

25

Set an inviting table with an Evergreen Spray Tablecloth and Acorn Napkins. Crewel yarn gives the embroidery a natural texture. For placecards, add name tags to the napkin rings.

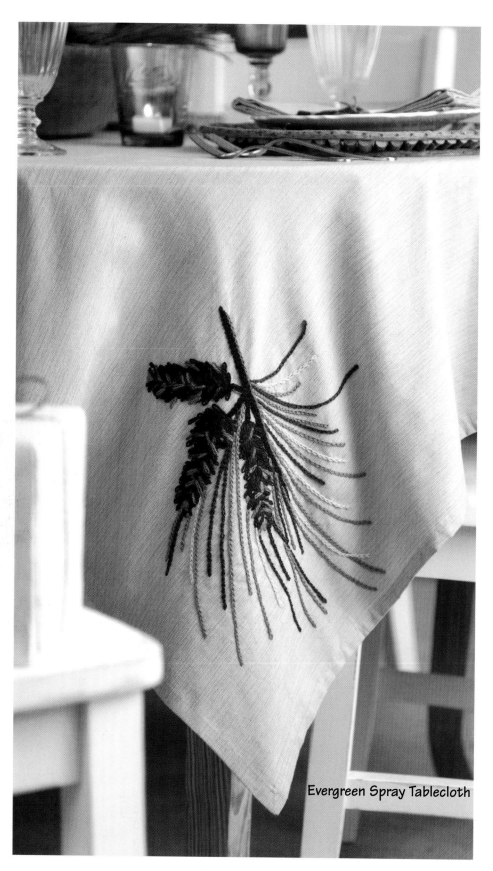

Evergreen Spray Tablecloth

Evergreen Spray Tablecloth
- tissue paper
- tablecloth
- grey, dark grey, dark brown, very light olive, olive and dark olive 2-ply wool crewel yarn

Read Embroidery Stitches on pages 138-139 before beginning.

Enlarge the pattern (page 146) to 140%. Use the enlarged pattern to transfer (page 137) the design to the tablecloth corners. Using 1 ply of yarn, work *Chain Stitches* for the needles and branches and *Lazy Daisy* pinecones.

Acorn Napkin
- tissue paper
- napkin
- gold, golden brown, dark brown and olive 2-ply wool crewel yarn
- dark brown felt
- 3/8" and 7/8" dia. buttons
- tag
- rickrack
- snowflake charm
- craft glue
- alphabet stickers

Read Embroidery Stitches on pages 138-139 before beginning.

1. Transfer (page 137) the pattern (page 145) to a napkin. Using 1 ply of yarn, work *Chain Stitches* for the acorn bottom and cap outline and *Bullion Knots* for the acorn caps.
2. For the napkin ring, work olive *Chain Stitches* along the center of a 1 1/2"x12" dark brown felt piece. Finish with a large loop closure and sew the large button to the other end. Fasten the napkin ring around the folded napkin.
3. Glue felt, rickrack and the snowflake charm to a tag. Personalize with stickers. Tie the small button to the tag with yarn and loop over the napkin ring button.

Acorn Napkin

Wrapped Packages

No snow outside? Let it snow inside! A purchased snowflake garland adds the beauty of the season to Wrapped Packages. Make a curtain of "falling" snow with Window Dressing Garlands. They're simple to create by cutting snowflakes from felt and adding buttons and pom-poms.

Wrapped Packages

Unique wrappings conceal special holiday gifts. Mix and match handmade papers, brown kraft paper, ribbon, snowflake garland, wide twill tape, buttons, felt snowflakes (enlarge patterns on page 143 as desired), string and baby rickrack as you wrap each box.

Create a keepsake tag ornament by embroidering a mistletoe stem (pattern, page 145) with embroidery floss on a felt tag. We used 2 strands of floss to work *Chain Stitches* (page 139) for the stem, *Stem Stitch* leaves and *Straight Stitch* leaf veins. Add *French Knot* berries with 4 floss strands.

Window Dressing Garlands
Instructions are on page 118.

Window Dressing Garlands

CHRISTMAS *Fun* and GAMeS

These ideas for decorations and children's toys are sure to be fun for everyone! In fact, lots of grownups will recognize the vintage building toys and board game pieces in this playful collection of tree ornaments. The stuffed toy Horsie and Piggie are simple to sew and will become a child's best pals. Whether you create this Christmas theme for the playroom or the living room, you'll have a wonderful time enjoying the whimsy of the season, right along with the kids!

Fun & Games Tree instructions are on page 118.

Piggie
Horsie

Horsie

- 18"x29" piece of striped knit fabric cut from a gently used T-shirt
- two 20"x24" pieces of green lightweight knit fabric cut from a gently used sweater
- one 17"x28" and two 19"x23" pieces of lightweight fusible interfacing
- fabric marking pen
- paper-backed fusible web
- blue and green felt

- 5 small plastic zipping bags loosely filled with dried beans
- polyester fiberfill
- medium weight yarn (we used green, red, yellow and blue)
- brown and green embroidery floss

(continued on page 119)

Piggie
Instructions are on page 120.

The cute & cuddly Horsie and Piggie are sewn from gently worn sweaters and a T-shirt or print fabric. Gift Cubes are colorful and sturdy, and can be used all year for floor pillows or handy ottomans. Too cold to play outside? A few games of Turtle Tic-Tac-Toe Toss will keep youngsters warm and happy indoors.

Gift Cubes
- 22"x22"x4" piece of Nu-Foam® Densified Polyester
- spray adhesive
- 3/4 yard *each* of red and blue baby wale corduroy
- fabric marking pen
- 5 yards of 1 1/2" wide ribbon
- 2" dia. pom-poms (1 red and 1 green)
- craft glue

Match right sides, raw edges and use a 1/2" seam allowance for all sewing.

1. Cut Nu-Foam into four 11"x11"x4" pieces. Stack two pieces together to measure 11"x11"x8"; then, adhere the layers with spray adhesive to make a foam cube. Repeat with the remaining pieces.

2. Cut 2 squares 12"x12" and 4 rectangles 12"x9" **each** from red and blue corduroy. Mark a dot 1/2" from each corner on the wrong side of each square and rectangle.

(continued on page 120)

Turtle Tic-Tac-Toe Toss
Instructions begin on page 118.

Gift Cubes

Turtle Tic-Tac-Toe Toss

Holiday Words Ornaments
- wood letter tiles and trays (we used pieces from a vintage Scrabble® game)
- fine-tooth handsaw
- sandpaper
- acrylic paint and paintbrush
- wood glue
- wood spools (we used vintage Tinkertoys®)
- wood beads (assorted sizes and colors)
- 6-ply multi-colored hemp twine

1. Cut the letter trays to fit the desired holiday words. Sand the cut ends and paint the trays.
2. Glue letters on the trays.
3. For each hanger, thread and glue beads and/or spools to center of a twine length. Glue the hanger ends to either side of the letter trays.

Personalized Tree Ornaments
Bead Garland
Star Ornament/Tree Topper
Instructions begin on page 120.

Personalized Tree Ornaments

Bead Garland

Star Ornament/Tree Topper

Holiday Words Ornaments

If the Holiday Words Ornaments look familiar, it's because they use wood tiles from a popular board game! The kids will enjoy stringing a Bead Garland and using pieces of a wood toy construction set to make Personalized Tree Ornaments, Star Ornaments and a Tree Topper. We used infant's and toddler's socks on the colorful Sock Garland, while the red bow on the yarn-wrapped Wreath is fashioned from two pairs of socks!

Memory is the treasury and guardian of all things.
@-MARCUS TULLIUS CICERO·

Sock Garland
Wreath

Sock Garland

Thread a large sharp needle with yarn and knot one end. Sew favorite infant and toddler socks to a ³/₈" wide ribbon length with a single stitch; knot close to the ribbon and cut the yarn. Glue pom-poms to the ribbon between the socks. Make a few of these garlands and hang with thumbtacks for a quick and whimsical wall decoration!

Wreath

This fun wreath made of yarn, wooden blocks and 2 pairs of toddler knee socks is oh-so-easy to make. Simply wrap and glue assorted colors and lengths of yarn around a foam wreath. Drill a hole through the center of wood alphabet blocks that spell JOY. Leaving the tying yarn at least 30" long, make a 3" diameter pom-pom (page 140). Place the pom-pom under the block stack and run the tying yarn up through the holes. Knot the yarn around the wreath and trim the ends. Tie the socks into a bow and glue to the wreath.

'Tis the season to Sew

Oh, how time flies when you're stitching these sweet projects! Vintage and reproduction fabrics are "sew" very merry when used to make a Blooming Apron, adorable Farmgirl Doll, or Mini Pennant Swag. Give your Christmas décor a fresh look this year by whipping up a whole garden of quick & colorful flower ornaments! They're truly simple to create for the tree, for package decorations and more.

Blooming Apron instructions are on page 123.

Blooming Apron

Blooming Tree Skirt

- 40"x40" square of fabric
- string
- water-soluble fabric marker
- thumb tack
- 1 yard fabric for ruffle
- 3⅜ yards ball fringe
- large and small gathered fabric ornaments

When sewing, always match right sides and raw edges and use a ½" seam allowance.

1. For the skirt, follow *Making a Fabric Circle* (page 137) and use a 19" string measurement to mark the outer cutting line on the fabric square. Remove the tack and use a 1" string measurement to mark the inner cutting line.

2. Cut through all fabric layers along the drawn lines. Unfold the circle. Cut a back opening from the outer edge to the center opening. Press the center opening and the back opening edges ¼" to the wrong side twice, clipping as necessary; topstitch.

3. Cut a 5"x240" strip for the ruffle, piecing as necessary. Matching the long, raw edges, fold the ruffle in half and sew the ends. Turn right side out and press. Baste along the raw edge at ½" and ¼"; pull the basting threads, gathering the ruffle to fit the outer edge of the skirt. Sew the ruffle to the skirt outer edge. Press the seam allowances toward the skirt.

4. Sew the fringe over the ruffle seam, turning the ends ½" to the wrong side.

5. Pin large and small gathered fabric ornaments to the tree skirt.

Button Wreath

Blooming Tree Skirt

Who says you can't have a flower garden in December? These fabric flowers are so simple, you can "grow" dozens in a single afternoon! Use your favorite buttons or make covered buttons for quick flower centers. Let the finished flowers blossom on a Christmas tree. Add them to a Blooming Tree Skirt that's trimmed with a ruffle and pom-poms. You'll find lots of ways to color your holidays with these fast little floral projects, and you don't even need a green thumb!

Felt Flower Ornament

Gathered Fabric Ornament

Felt Flower Ornament
• fabric and felt scraps
• paper-backed fusible web
• scallop-edged scissors
• 7/8" dia. self-covered button
• small clothespin
• craft glue

1. Fuse web to the wrong side of a fabric scrap.
2. Enlarge the patterns (page 141) to 200%. Using the enlarged patterns, cut the circle from felt with the scallop-edged scissors and the flower from the web-backed fabric. Fuse the flower to the circle.
3. Cut a 4" diameter fabric circle. Follow *Making Yo-Yo's* (page 140) to make a yo-yo. Cover the button with fabric. Sew the yo-yo and button to the flower center. Glue the clothespin to the flower back.

Gathered Fabric Ornament
• 1 1/2"x22" fabric strip (or a 2"x55" fabric strip for a large ornament)
• matching embroidery floss
• button
• fabric scrap for large ornament center
• felt scrap
• small clothespin
• craft glue

1. For a small ornament, use floss to work *Running Stitches* (page 139) along 1 long edge of the fabric strip. Pull the thread to tightly gather the strip into a circle; knot the thread. Sew the button to the circle center.
2. Glue the flower to a 1 1/2" diameter felt circle. Glue the clothespin to the flower back.
3. For a large ornament, follow Steps 1-2 using a 2"x55" fabric strip, a 2 3/4" diameter felt circle and *Making A Yo-Yo* (page 140) from a 4" diameter fabric circle for the flower center. Sew the yo-yo and button to the flower.

Flower Ornament/Tree Topper

Gathered Rickrack Ornament

Button Wreath
Flower Ornament/Tree Topper
Gathered Rickrack Ornament
Instructions begin on page 121.

39

Your fabric scraps will look amazing on an easy Mini Pennant Swag. If you like to use baskets for storage caddies, make them pretty with Basket Liners. The liner for round baskets has a drawstring top, which is great for keeping the contents dust-free. You surely know a little girl (or a big girl!) who would love to have her very own Farmgirl Doll with braided yarn hair and an embroidered smile. The Blooming Apron is a charming way to color your Christmas with happy, springtime hues.

Basket Liners

- small basket
- fabric to line basket
- cotton yarn
- ribbon for round basket
- felt flower or gathered fabric ornament (page 39)

Rectangular Basket

When sewing, always match right sides and raw edges and use a 1/4" seam allowance.

1. To line a rectangular basket, measure the basket inside bottom width and length; add 1/2" to each measurement and cut a fabric piece this size. Measure the height of the basket and add 2". Measure around the basket and add 1". Cut a fabric piece this size.

2. Matching the short ends, sew the larger fabric piece into a ring. Placing the seam at one corner, sew the ring to the fabric bottom. Press the top raw edge 1/2" to the wrong side and topstitch. Place the liner in the basket and mark the handles on the liner. Slit the liner open just enough to allow the fabric to fold over the basket top and lie flat. Beginning at each side of the slit, use yarn to work *Running Stitches* (page 139) near the edge; tie yarn ends in bows and clip on a felt flower ornament.

Round Basket

When sewing, always match right sides and raw edges and use a 1/4" seam allowance.

1. To line a round basket with a drawstring-style liner, measure the basket inside bottom diameter; add 1/2" and cut a fabric circle this size. Measure the height of the basket and add 5". Measure around the basket top and add 1". Cut a fabric piece this size. Cut 2 fabric pieces 2 1/4"x half the basket top measurement plus 1"; set these 2 pieces aside.

2. Matching the short ends, sew the larger rectangular fabric piece into a ring. Sew the ring to the fabric circle. For the casing, press the top raw edge 1/2" to the wrong side and topstitch. Remove the stitching from side seam above the casing line. Thread a ribbon length through the casing.

3. For the basket cuff, press 1/2" to the wrong side on both ends and 1 long edge of each of the remaining fabric pieces, forming a casing at the bottom; topstitch. Matching the right sides, pin, then stitch the fabric pieces to the basket liner 3 1/2" below the liner top edge. Thread a yarn length through each casing.

4. Place the liner in the basket, arrange the cuff around the handle and tie the yarn ends in a bow; clip on a gathered flower.

Mini Pennant Swag
Farmgirl Doll
Blooming Apron
Instructions begin on page 123.

Mini Pennant Swag

Basket Liners

Farmgirl Doll

Blooming Apron   41

inspirations

The holiday spirit is easy to see in these innovative ideas! Paper birds seem to flutter from their vintage birdcages to the branches of a glittering tree. Easy-to-paint plates, tag sale bottles, and delightful old ornaments add plenty of sparkle, too. You'll find ideas for felt stockings, advent calendars the kids will adore and merry wreaths. There are also more than a dozen ways to make your heartfelt gifts more festive with handmade wraps and tags. Look through these pages and let this jolly collection of projects inspire your creative Christmas spirit!

All Aflutter instructions are on page 125.

All Aflutter

Shiny & Bright

44

You never know what wonderful things you'll discover at tag sales! The Country Friends found a way to add well-loved dishes and ornaments to the décor with the Shiny & Bright holiday display. Place your bottle collection on a windowsill, add a tree topper collection and a winter scene, and see how pretty it all looks Through the Window.

Shiny & Bright

Create a colorful holiday display by placing vintage ornaments of all shapes and sizes in clear glass apothecary jars. Use paints suitable for ceramics to stencil (page 137) flea market plates (patterns on page 152; size them to fit your plates). Freehand paint the greenery details. Embellish a plate by hanging a unique glass ball with twill tape. Add a few greens and some ribbon to complete this vignette.

Through the Window

A snow-covered hillside (page 149, sized to fit your window) is a scenic backdrop for a collection of wintry figures. Cut a stencil (page 137) using the enlarged pattern and stencil the design on the window with spray snow. Dress up the sill with a collection of interesting bottles, delicate tree toppers and glass balls.

Christmas Favorites

Through the Window

Santa will be thrilled to see all these felt stockings waiting to be filled. Wool roving makes Santa's beard fluffy. The Tree is from a printed tablecloth that once was sadly stained, but is now part of a cheery stocking. Quick appliqué brings the Bird and leaves to life, while Poinsettias bloom from easy embroidery!

Stockings
Santa
- two 14"x23" pieces of aqua felt
- dressmaker's tracing paper
- red, ivory, peach, pink and black wool roving
- needle felting tool and mat
- 3/4" dia. shank button for nose
- fabric glue
- 16"x8" piece of chenille fabric
- 16" length of ball fringe

1. Enlarge the pattern (page 151) to 206%. Using the enlarged pattern, cut 2 aqua felt stocking pieces. Using dressmaker's tracing paper, transfer the design to 1 piece. For the hanger, cut a 1"x5" felt piece.

2. Follow *Needle Felting* (pages 139-140) to fill in Santa. For the moustache, needle felt a roving piece above the mouth, leaving the ends loose. Sew Santa's button nose in place. Add ivory roving "snow" to the stocking.

3. Leaving the top open, glue the stocking pieces together along the edges. Fold under 1/4" along both long edges and 1 short end of the chenille piece. Overlap the short ends and glue, forming a ring. Use *Running Stitches* (page 139) to gather the chenille piece to about 3 1/2" high. Glue the fringe to the chenille piece bottom edge. Glue the chenille piece top edge to the stocking top, gluing the hanger in the upper right corner.

Tree
Instructions are on page 125.

Stockings

Bird
- two 14"x23" pieces of red felt
- fabric scraps
- paper-backed fusible web
- embroidery floss
- buttons
- clear nylon thread

1. Enlarge the Bird patterns (page 148) to 200%. Enlarge the Poinsettias Stocking pattern (page 150, ignoring the poinsettia design) to 206%. Using the enlarged stocking pattern, cut 2 red felt stocking pieces. For the hanger, cut a 1"x5" felt piece.

2. Fuse web to the back of each fabric scrap. Using the enlarged Bird patterns, cut body, wing, 5 small leaf and 5 large leaf appliqués. Fuse the appliqués to 1 stocking piece. Use floss to work a *Running Stitch* (page 139) vine, a French Knot eye and to sew on the buttons.

3. Leaving the top open, use nylon thread to sew the stocking pieces together along the edges, catching the hanger in the upper right corner.

Poinsettias

- two 14"x23" pieces of blue felt
- tissue paper
- tan crewel wool
- ivory and tan textured yarns
- fabric glue

Read Embroidery Stitches on pages 138-139 before beginning.

1. Enlarge the pattern (page 150) to 206%. Using the enlarged pattern, cut 2 blue felt stocking pieces. For the hanger, cut a 1"x5" felt piece.

2. *Transfer* (page 137) the design to 1 felt stocking. Embroider the design using the crewel wool for the *Chain Stitches, Straight Stitches* and small *French Knots.* Work additional larger *French Knot* flower centers with the ivory textured yarn.

3. Using crewel wool, work *Couching Stitches* and *French Knots* to attach lengths of ivory and tan yarn to the cuff and toe. Leaving the top open, glue the stocking pieces together along the edges, gluing the hanger in the upper right corner.

Counting the Days

Advent Calendars bring out the kid in everyone. That's because we all remember the excitement of counting the days 'til Christmas! With these ideas, you can track the days with colorful tags, bags of candy and other treats or a variety of clever magnets with fun messages hidden underneath.

Advent Calendars
A Jolly Christmas Countdown

A simple enamel-ware tray is transformed into a countdown to Christmas with fun magnets. Make magnets from cardstock, tags, covered buttons, dominos, dice, vintage tags and wrappings, rub-on numbers, rubber stamps, playing cards, small numeral stencils and all kinds of scrapbooking supplies. Place a small printed reward, such as "Bake cookies with Mom," under each magnet.

Counting the Days
Matchbox Garland
Mini Gift Sacks
Instructions begin on page 125.

Matchbox Garland

Mini Gift Sacks

A Jolly Christmas Countdown

It is LATER

DEC. 23rd

than you think.

Wouldn't it be merry to have a wreath on every door in your home? If you don't have time to make all four of these Whimsical Wreaths, most are so simple that you can surely create one for your front door! With just a little more time, you could make two of the same kind and give the second one as a gift!

Whimsical Wreaths

Vintage Angels

Dress up a plain 12" greenery wreath by wiring vintage ceramic angel bells along the bottom. Complete the wreath with layered circles (punched from cardstock and favorite holiday cards), vintage ornaments and a twill tape bow.

Monogrammed Apple

Thread apples (fresh or artificial) on a sturdy 12" wire ring (cut open with wire cutters). Cover a wooden or chipboard letter with scrapbook paper and lightly sand the edges. Glue a craft stick to the letter back and insert into the bottom apple. Glue a small wood block behind the letter to keep it from tilting. Hang the wreath from a pretty ribbon.

Felt Poinsettia

Begin by wiring pinecones to a 16" wire wreath form (we used an artificial pinecone garland). Enlarge the poinsettia pattern (page 148) to 200% and use it to cut 21 petals from assorted red felted wool and wool felt; cut 9 leaves from green wool felt. For each poinsettia, sew 7 petals together at the center; sew a button to the center. Hot glue the poinsettias and leaves to the pinecone wreath.

Burlap Holly

Enlarge the Mini Pennant Swag holly leaf pattern (page 141) to 215% and 275%. Use the smaller pattern to cut 14 fabric leaves; use the larger pattern to cut 23 burlap leaves. Drybrush (page 138) the burlap leaf edges with green acrylic paint. Layer the fabric leaves on some of the burlap leaves. Work embroidery floss Running Stitches (page 139) through the leaf centers. Sew buttons to felt rounds. Glue the leaves, felt-backed buttons and letter squares to a burlap-wrapped 14" foam wreath. Add a wide twill tape bow to the wreath top.

Vintage Angels

Monogrammed Apple

Felt Poinsettia

Burlap Holly

Wraps & Tags
Special Cards

So that we may always see Christmas through a child's eyes, add color to photocopies of favorite photos from years past before attaching to simple cardstock cards. A few stickers or some rub-ons create a card that is simply perfect.

For those holiday gift cards or even cash, enlarge the holder patterns (page 149) to 200%. Transfer the pattern to scrapbook paper and cut out. Fold the paper along the dashed lines. Place the gift inside the holder and trim with ribbons, stickers and tags.

Box of Tags

Purchased shipping tags, backed with patterned cardstock, are the perfect size for Christmas trees fashioned from ribbon and rickrack or vintage wrapping paper. Attach a simple or fancy button topper (add a rub-on holiday message, if you'd like) and a ribbon at the top. Decorate a leftover greeting card box with more ribbon and rickrack and you've got a great hostess or Secret Santa gift.

Handmade Boxes
Menswear Gift Sacks
Instructions begin on page 126.

Box of Tags

52

Handmade Boxes

This collection of Wraps & Tags offers original ways to present special gifts. Tuck a surprise in a gift bag or box, or simply include a one-of-a-kind card that's pretty enough to hang on the tree. With a Box of Tags, you can even make a thoughtful gift of your handcrafted creations.

Menswear Gift Sacks

Handmade Gifts

Surprise your nearest & dearest with this assortment of wonderful handmade gifts. Anyone who's young at heart will love a Snow Day Pillow that celebrates the fun of a fresh snowfall. Help a beginning stitcher by creating a Yo-Yo Sewing Kit and a Blossoming Pincushion. A Cozy Cottage Night Light will make a merry glow. From darling Silhouette Ornaments to a handy Coiled Rag Basket, you'll find lots of great ideas for all the names on your gift list!

Snow Day Pillow instructions are on page 128.

Snow Day Pillow

Delight little ones with a Christmas Bib, appliquéd Tractor Hat and a zany Mitten Puppet. For someone a little older, it's easy to fashion a Vintage Fabric Scarf. As an option to crocheting the edging, you can sew on rickrack, instead.

Tractor Hat
- child's knit hat
- paper-backed fusible web
- fabric scraps for appliqués and ear flaps
- 5"x4" felt piece to match hat
- clear nylon thread
- embroidery floss
- size 2 snap
- yarn to match hat
- crochet hook

(continued on page 128)

Mitten Puppet
Instructions are on page 129.

Christmas Bib

Tractor Hat

Mitten Puppet

56

Christmas Bib

- fabric strips of varying widths (we used 8 different fabrics)
- 11"x14" fabric piece for backing
- twill tape or ribbon with holiday message
- liquid fray preventative
- ½" dia. hole punch
- felt scrap
- hook and loop fastener

Always match right sides and use a ¼" seam allowance when sewing.

1. Match the long edges and sew the fabric strips together for the bib front.
2. Enlarge the pattern (page 157) to 200%. Using the enlarged pattern, cut the bib front and backing.
3. Apply fray preventative to the twill tape ends. Layer and attach 2 punched felt circles and the twill tape to the bib front.
4. Leaving an opening for turning, sew the bib front and back together. Clip the curves, turn right side out and press. Sew the opening closed. Sew the fastener to the bib center back.

Vintage Fabric Scarf
Instructions are on page 129.

Vintage Fabric Scarf

Big, Beautiful Tote

Someone you know needs an extra bag to carry large projects and necessities. The Big, Beautiful Tote will do the job with flair, and it's a great chance to sew with your favorite fabrics! If you'd like to create Charming Jewelry, look in the attic or take in a tag sale to find small items such as buttons, earrings and crocheted flowers. Add little charms to make your necklace oh-so sweet!

Big, Beautiful Tote
- ⅝ yard brown fabric
- ⅛ yard **each** of 12 different fabrics for stripes
- ¾ yard fabric for lining
- 1¾ yards lightweight fusible interfacing
- rotary ruler with a 60° line, rotary cutter and cutting mat
- 4½"x13½" piece of cardboard

Always match right sides and use a ½" seam allowance when sewing, unless otherwise indicated.

1. From the lining fabric, cut two 19"x17" pieces and two 14½"x5½" pieces. Fuse interfacing to the wrong side of the larger pieces and set aside.

2. From the brown fabric, cut two 19"x7¾" bottom pieces, two 24"x4" strap pieces and four 19"x2" top pieces. Center and fuse a 3"x23" interfacing strip to the wrong side of each strap. Fuse interfacing to the wrong side of top pieces; set aside.

(continued on page 130)

Charming Jewelry

Necklace

- assorted buttons
- flat charm bases
- E-6000® jewelry and craft adhesive
- wire cutters
- assorted beads
- head pins and eye pins
- needle-nose jewelry pliers
- jump rings
- crocheted or knitted flowers (we found ours in Grandma's attic)
- assorted charms (we used key charms)
- necklace chain (ours is 30" long)
- vintage clip-style earring
- assorted ribbons

1. For the button charms, use wire cutters to remove any shanks from buttons and glue to the charm bases.

2. For the bead dangles, thread beads onto head pins and eye pins. Follow *Shaping Eye Loops* (page 140) to connect beads to one another.

3. Sew buttons to the flower centers.

4. Follow *Using Jump Rings* (page 140) to attach the charms, bead dangles and button charms to the necklace chain. Sew the flowers to the necklace and clip a few ribbons to the necklace with the earring.

Ring

Cut the shank from a vintage button with wire cutters; then, glue the button to an adjustable ring base.

Charming Jewelry

Silhouette Ornament

- profile photo of child
- tracing paper
- transfer paper
- flat circle clear glass ornament
- black acrylic paint and paintbrush
- assorted ribbons
- jeweled brad

1. Trace the child's profile and size the image to fit on the ornament. Use transfer paper to transfer the outline to the ornament back. Paint the image black.
2. Tie ribbon to the ornament top and add the brad. Attach a ribbon hanger.

Silhouette Ornament

Cozy Cottage Night Light

Create a holiday cottage night light by painting and decorating a purchased unfinished wood house (ours is 9" high). First, paint the house with acrylic paints; then, use finishing nails to attach an aluminum flashing roof and trim it with rickrack "snow." The dormer roof, shutters and colorful trees are all cut from patterned cardstock. Buttons, a mini wreath and mica flakes along the window and door top edges are a sweet touch. Insert a 7-watt single light cord into a hole drilled in the house back to get that cozy glow.

Cozy Cottage Night Light

For a gift that will touch her heart, why not present Grandma with Silhouette Ornaments featuring the profiles of her grandchildren? A Cozy Cottage Night Light will spread the cheery spirit of the season. And of course, the more the merrier…especially when it comes to the buttons you add to the Framed Button Tree! It's a fun project for everyone, from school-age kids to adults.

Framed Button Tree
- frame with a 12"x16" back opening
- paper-backed fusible web
- 12"x14" piece of felted wool
- 16"x20" fabric piece for background
- assorted vintage buttons
- 12"x16" piece of foam core board
- craft glue
- vintage Christmas pin (we used a jumping jack Santa)
- ribbon to decorate frame (optional)

1. Fuse the web to the wrong side of the wool fabric. Enlarge the pattern (page 152) to 200%. Using the enlarged pattern, cut the tree from the wool. Center and fuse the tree on the background fabric. Sew the buttons to the tree.
2. Center the foam core board on the wrong side of the background fabric. Wrap and glue the excess fabric to the board back.
3. Insert the board into the frame. Add a vintage Christmas pin and enhance the frame molding with ribbon if desired.

Framed Button Tree

61

Yo-Yo Sewing Kit

- 14"x14" piece of fabric
- 6"x10" piece of fabric for lining
- 5"x9" piece of fusible interfacing
- thick cardboard
- two 1⅛" dia. buttons
- ⅛"w ribbon
- wool felt scrap
- size 2 snap

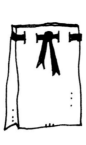

1. Cut a 6"x10" rectangle and two 5½" circles from fabric. Follow *Making Yo-Yo's* (page 140) to make 2 yo-yo's, placing a 2½" cardboard circle in the center of each yo-yo before gathering. Sew a button to each yo-yo with ribbon; set aside.

(continued on page 131)

Yo-Yo Sewing Kit

What cute & clever ways to keep sewing supplies at hand! The Yo-Yo Sewing Kit has a felt needle holder and room for small items your stitching friend may need. With a miniature pail for its base and a few colorful beaded pins, the Blossoming Pincushion is whimsical and bright!

Blossoming Pincushion

- mini pail (ours is 2¹/₂" high)
- 8"x8" felt square for petals
- 8"x8" fabric square for center
- polyester fiberfill
- hot glue gun
- glass head pins and beads
- jewelry adhesive
- cardstock tag and stickers
- ribbon

1. Enlarge the pattern (page 155) to 200%. Using the enlarged pattern, cut the flower petals from felt.
2. For the flower center, cut a 7" fabric circle (page 137). Work *Running Stitches* (page 139) ¹/₄" from the edge, place fiberfill in the center and tightly gather the circle; knot the thread.
3. Stuff the pail about ¹/₂ full with fiberfill. Center the felt petals and flower center in the pail. Hot glue securely in the pail.
4. For the beaded pins, use jewelry adhesive to glue beads on the pins. Adhere the stickers to the tag and tie to the pail handle.

Blossoming Pincushion

Every Christmas gift looks more festive with a bow! The Bow-Tied Apron is a snap to sew. It's also easy to add a monogram to a Hostess Towel (don't forget the ribbon bow and buttons). You'll be amazed at how quickly you can sew a Coiled Rag Basket, and it will look so pretty when piled high with bow-topped presents!

Bow-Tied Apron

- 30"x4" fabric piece for upper band
- 30"x12" fabric piece apron skirt
- 1³/₈ yards of fabric for waistband, ties and lining
- 1³/₄ yards of jumbo rickrack

Always match right sides and use a ¹/₂" seam allowance when sewing.

1. Cut a 30"x17" fabric piece for the lining, two 5"x44" fabric pieces for the ties and a 30"x3" fabric piece for the waistband.

2. For the apron front, sew the upper band and apron skirt pieces together along one long edge. Cut two 30" lengths of rickrack. Baste a length along the upper band raw edge and near the bottom edge of the apron skirt. Sew the waistband to the upper band.

3. For each tie, sew the long edges and one short end together, angling the end. Clip the corners, turn right side out and press. Matching the raw edges, pin one tie to each side of the waistband. Sew the lining to the apron front, leaving an opening for turning. Clip the corners, turn right side out and press. Sew the opening closed.

Bow-Tied Apron

Coiled Rag Basket

Hostess Towel

Make a quick hostess gift for each holiday party on your calendar. Print or draw a 4" high letter. Transfer the letter to a fabric piece that has been backed with fusible web. Cut out the letter, fuse it to a linen tea towel and zigzag along the raw edges. Use clear nylon thread to sew ribbon along the towel bottom edge. Add buttons and a bow and you're done!

Coiled Rag Basket

Instructions are on page 131.

Hostess Towel

Sweet and Savory Gifts of the Season

If you enjoy baking cookies, making pies and cakes or tossing together a simple but savory snack, you'll love these ideas for gifts from the kitchen! Help a busy cook serve a heavenly dessert with Blueberry Cream Coffee Cake in a festive Cake Box. Make Mock Cherry Pies and place them in a Pie Basket for a special neighbor. For a gift that's as pretty as it is delicious, present a Parfait Glass Bouquet arranged with Mint Cookies & Cream Truffle Pops. With fourteen delicious recipes and plenty of gift-giving ideas, finding the perfect presents for everyone just became a lot easier!

Blueberry Cream Coffee Cake

A traditional recipe, but still a favorite of mine!

²/₃ c. plus 2 T. sugar, divided
¹/₄ c. butter, softened
1 egg
¹/₄ t. lemon extract
1 c. plus 3 T. all-purpose flour, divided
1¹/₂ t. baking powder
¹/₂ t. salt
¹/₂ t. cinnamon, divided
¹/₂ c. milk
1 c. blueberries
4 oz. cream cheese, cubed
1 T. cold butter

Blend together ²/₃ cup sugar and butter until light and fluffy. Blend in egg and lemon extract. In a separate bowl, combine one cup flour, baking powder, salt and ¹/₄ teaspoon cinnamon. Add alternately with milk to creamed mixture. Toss blueberries with one tablespoon flour, fold in batter with cream cheese and pour into greased and floured 9" springform pan.

To prepare topping, combine remaining 2 tablespoons sugar, 2 tablespoons flour and ¹/₄ teaspoon cinnamon. Cut in butter until mixture resembles coarse crumbs. Sprinkle evenly over batter. Bake at 375 degrees for 30 minutes or until cake tests done. Makes 6 servings.

Stephanie Moon
Boise, ID

Cake Box instructions are on page 132.

67

A Chip & Dip Mix Container of Baked Pita Chips includes Santa's Zesty Mix for dip. Cocoa-Cherry Macaroons are even sweeter when packaged in the Macaroons 4 U! Box. The Rustic Apple Tart is fun to present with a button-trimmed Card!

Baked Pita Chips

Chewier and fresher-tasting than bagged chips.

8 6" round pita breads
2 T. olive oil
1 t. garlic powder

Split pita bread rounds. Brush cut sides with olive oil, then cut into 6 wedges. Sprinkle with garlic powder and bake in a single layer at 350 degrees for 10 to 12 minutes, or until crisp. Store in airtight container. Makes 8 dozen.

Santa's Zesty Mix

1 T. dried chives
1 t. garlic salt
½ t. dill weed
½ t. paprika
⅛ t. onion powder

Combine ingredients in a small bowl; spoon into a small clear plastic zipping bag. Seal; use within 6 months. Attach instructions.

Instructions: Combine mix with one tablespoon lemon juice, one cup mayonnaise, and one cup sour cream. Refrigerate until chilled. Makes 2 cups.

Chip & Dip Mix Container instructions are on page 132.

Cocoa-Cherry Macaroons

Tuck a dozen of these delights into a candy box for a sweet gift.

6 c. sweetened flaked coconut
14-oz. can sweetened condensed milk
1 t. vanilla extract
1 c. mini semi-sweet chocolate chips
½ c. maraschino cherries, drained and chopped

Combine coconut, condensed milk and vanilla in a large bowl; mix until coconut is well coated. Stir in chocolate chips and cherries. Drop by heaping teaspoonfuls 2 inches apart on a parchment paper-lined baking sheet. Bake at 350 degrees for 10 to 12 minutes. Makes 3 dozen.

Charity Meyer
Lewisberry, PA

Macaroons 4 U! Box instructions are on page 133.

Baked Pita Chips, Santa's Zesty Mix
Chip & Dip Mix Container

Cocoa-Cherry Macaroons
Macaroons 4 U! Box

Rustic Apple Tart
Card

Rustic Apple Tart

We like to use a combination of Granny Smith and Rome apples but substitute your favorites, if you'd like.

1³/₄ c. all-purpose flour
1 t. salt
²/₃ c. shortening, cut into small
    pieces
¹/₂ c. ice water
2 T. unsalted butter, cut into
    small pieces

Combine flour and salt; cut in shortening with a pastry blender until mixture resembles coarse meal. Sprinkle cold water, one tablespoon at a time, over surface; stir with a fork until dry ingredients are moistened. Press dough into 4-inch circle. Cover and chill at least one hour.

Roll dough into a 12-inch circle on a floured surface. Transfer dough onto a parchment-lined baking sheet. Spoon filling into center of dough and spread to the edges, leaving a 2-inch border. Dot with butter. Fold dough up and over the filling, pleating every 2 inches and leaving the center open. Gently press dough to seal the pleats. Chill 20 minutes.

Bake at 425 degrees on the lower third of the oven for 15 minutes. Reduce heat to 375 degrees and continue to bake 50 minutes or until crust is golden and the fruit is tender. Let tart stand 5 minutes on the baking sheet on a wire rack. Remove from baking sheet to a wire rack to cool completely. Makes 6 to 8 servings.

Filling:
2 c. peeled, cored and sliced
    Granny Smith apples
2 c. peeled, cored and sliced
    Rome apples
¹/₂ c. sugar
2 to 3 T. all-purpose flour
¹/₈ t. salt

Combine all ingredients in a large bowl.

Card instructions are on page 133.

good friends good food

69

Cherry Nut Cake

This moist and tender cake can be served for dessert or as a breakfast treat on Christmas morning.

1³/₄ c. cake flour
1¹/₂ t. baking powder
¹/₄ t. baking soda
¹/₂ t. salt
¹/₂ c. butter, softened
1 c. sugar
1 egg
1 egg white
³/₄ c. orange juice
³/₄ c. chopped pecans
¹/₂ c. cherries canned in water,
    drained and liquid reserved

Sift flour, baking powder, baking soda and salt together; set aside. Beat butter and sugar until fluffy; add egg and egg white and beat well. Gradually add flour mixture alternately with orange juice. Fold in pecans and cherries.

Pour into a greased and floured 6-cup Bundt® pan. Bake at 350 degrees for 45 to 50 minutes or until a toothpick inserted in center comes out clean. Cool on a wire rack for 5 minutes. Carefully run a knife around the edge of pan to loosen; cool completely on wire rack. Spoon Cherry Sauce over cake.

Cherry Sauce:
Juice from 14¹/₂-oz. can cherries in
    water
1 T. cornstarch
1 T. butter
21-oz. can cherry pie filling

Combine first 3 ingredients in a medium saucepan; heat over medium heat 3 minutes or until thickened. Stir in pie filling; cook one minute or until heated through.

Lucille Pulliam
Fort Smith, AR

A tangy sauce made with pie filling is the perfect topper for Cherry Nut Cake! When the sweet-and-salty goodness of A Merry Mix is all gone, the reusable Gift Box can be filled with more snacks. For a yummy present anyone will love, tuck a Pineapple & Nut Cheese Ball into a Cheese Ball Box.

THE CHRISTMAS BAKERY

Cherry Nut Cake

A Merry Mix

A crunchy snack with a southwestern kick.

1 c. mini pretzels
1 c. corn chips
1 c. oyster crackers
1 c. toasted pumpkin seeds
1 c. honey-roasted peanuts
2 T. butter, melted
2 T. brown sugar, packed
1 t. Worcestershire sauce
1 t. chili powder
1/2 t. onion salt
1/2 t. cumin
1/8 t. cayenne pepper

Toss the first 5 ingredients together in a large mixing bowl; set aside.

Whisk remaining ingredients together; pour over snack mix, stirring to coat. Spread mix in a roasting pan; bake at 300 degrees for 25 minutes, stirring after 12 minutes. Cool completely; store in an airtight container. Makes about 5 cups.

Gift Box instructions are on page 134.

**A Merry Mix
Gift Box**

**Pineapple & Nut Cheese Ball
Cheese Ball Box**

Pineapple & Nut Cheese Ball

This sweet and savory appetizer can be used for 2 gifts...or save one for yourself.

8-oz. pkg. cream cheese, softened
2 c. chopped pecans, divided
8-oz. can crushed pineapple, drained
1/4 c. green pepper, chopped
2 T. onion, chopped
2 t. seasoned salt

Beat cream cheese until smooth. Blend in one cup pecans and remaining ingredients. Shape into 2 balls; roll each ball in remaining pecans. Wrap in plastic wrap. Refrigerate until ready to serve. Makes 2 cheese balls.

*Michelle Campen
Peoria, IL*

Cheese Ball Box instructions are on page 134.

Cranberry Scones
Scone Cozy

Cranberry Scones

I've had this recipe for many years; it's a breakfast "must-have!"

2¹/₂ c. all-purpose flour
2¹/₂ t. baking powder
¹/₂ t. baking soda
³/₄ c. butter, sliced
1 c. cranberries, chopped
²/₃ c. sugar
³/₄ c. buttermilk

Mix flour, baking powder and baking soda together in a large mixing bowl; cut in butter until mixture resembles coarse crumbs. Stir in cranberries and sugar; add buttermilk, mixing until just blended. Divide dough in half; roll each portion into an 8-inch circle, about ¹/₂-inch thick, on a lightly floured surface. Cut each portion into 8 wedges; arrange wedges on ungreased baking sheets.

Bake at 400 degrees for 12 to 15 minutes; remove to a wire rack to cool. Drizzle glaze over the tops. Let stand until glaze is hardened. Wrap loosely in wax paper. Makes 16 servings.

Glaze:
²/₃ c. powdered sugar
1 T. warm water
¹/₄ t. vanilla extract

Combine ingredients; mix well, adding additional warm water until desired spreading consistency is achieved.

*Cathy Light
Sedro Woolley, WA*

Scone Cozy instructions begin on page 134.

Cranberry Scones, nestled in a festive Scone Cozy, are an irresistible sight. Bake a dish of Norwegian Rice Pudding and present it with Potholders. Or create an easy Candy Glass by filling a vintage tumbler with Chocolate Peanut Clusters.

Norwegian Rice Pudding

Take this creamy treat to your Christmas potluck and leave the ceramic bowl and potholders for your host.

4 c. milk
³/₄ c. long-cooking rice, uncooked
1 egg, beaten
¹/₂ c. whipping cream
³/₄ c. sugar
1 t. salt
1 t. all-purpose flour
Garnish: sliced almonds, cinnamon

Heat milk to just boiling in a medium saucepan; set aside.

Rinse rice with hot water. In a double boiler, combine hot milk and rice. Cover and cook over medium heat for one hour, or until rice is tender and milk is almost absorbed, stirring occasionally; let cool.

Combine egg, whipping cream, sugar, salt and flour. Stir egg mixture into cooled cooked rice. Pour into a one-quart ovenproof serving bowl or baking dish. Bake at 325 degrees for 30 minutes or until custard is set and edges begin to turn golden. Garnish pudding, if desired. Makes 10 to 12 servings.

Potholder instructions are on page 135.

Norwegian Rice Pudding
Potholder

Chocolate Peanut Clusters

These salty-sweet homemade confections make a large batch to share with many friends.

16-oz. jar dry-roasted salted peanuts
16-oz. jar dry-roasted unsalted peanuts
2 lbs. white melting chocolate,
   coarsely chopped
4 oz. sweet baking chocolate,
   coarsely chopped
2 c. semi-sweet chocolate chips

In a 5-quart slow cooker, combine all ingredients. Cover and cook on low setting for 3 hours. Stir and drop candy by heaping tablespoonfuls onto wax paper. Let cool completely. Makes about 3¹/₄ pounds.

Candy Glass instructions are on page 135.

Chocolate Peanut Clusters
Candy Glass

73

Parfait Glass Bouquet
- Mint Cookies & Cream Truffle Pops
- parfait glass
- foam cone to fit inverted in the glass
- mica flakes
- ribbons, twill tape and rickrack
- wooden skewers, cut into 6"-8" lengths
- hot glue gun
- rub-on letters
- buttons

1. Place the foam in the glass and cover with mica flakes. Insert the pops in the cone.
2. For each festive "flag," wrap one or 2 ribbon, rickrack or twill tape 6" lengths around the end of a skewer; glue in place. Fill in between the pops with the flags.
3. For a clever tag, glue two 12" twill tape lengths to the end of a skewer. Add a rub-on message near the free end of one length and glue buttons to both pieces. Insert near the front of the glass.

Mint Cookies & Cream
Truffle Pops
Parfait Glass Bouquet

Mint Cookies & Cream Truffle Pops
These festive pops will be loved by kids and adults alike.

8-oz. pkg. cream cheese, softened
4 c. mint chocolate sandwich cookies, crushed
2 c. white chocolate chips
1 T. shortening

Beat cream cheese with a mixer until fluffy; blend in crushed cookies. Refrigerate for 2 hours. Roll dough into one-inch balls. Melt white chocolate chips with shortening in a double boiler over medium heat. Dip balls into mixture to coat. Place on wax paper to set; press ends of 6- to 8-inch wooden skewers into flat sides of balls. Wrap with cellophane and decorate with festive ribbons. Makes 2½ dozen.

Mock Cherry Pies
Pie Basket

What thoughtful gifts! A Parfait Glass Bouquet is as fun to make as it is to receive, and everyone will enjoy the Mint Cookies & Cream Truffle Pops it holds. Cranberries are sweet-tart treats when baked with raisins in Mock Cherry Pies. The liner in the Pie Basket is "oh-sew-simple."

Mock Cherry Pies

We suggest serving these miniature pies with a big dollop of vanilla ice cream.

2 c. cranberries, halved
1 c. raisins, chopped
2 c. sugar
1/4 c. all-purpose flour
2 T. butter, melted
1 t. vanilla extract
1/2 t. almond extract
1 c. boiling water
14.1-oz. pkg. refrigerated pie
    crusts

Combine all ingredients but pie crusts in a large bowl. Cut each pie crust into two 6 1/2-inch circles, reserving scraps. Place in four 4 1/2-inch pie plates. Divide cranberry mixture evenly over pie crusts in pie plates.

Cut reserved scraps into 1/2-inch wide strips. Lay strips at 1/2-inch intervals; fold back alternate strips as you weave crosswise strips over and under. Trim crusts even with outer rim of pie plates. Dampen edge of crusts with water; fold over strips, seal and crimp. Bake at 375 degrees for 30 minutes or until crust is golden and filling is bubbly. Cool in pans on wire racks. Makes 4 small pies.

Pie Basket instructions begin on page 135.

Oatmeal Coconut Chocolate Chip Cookies

These chocolate-studded cookies bake up into crispy bake-shop style treats.

It isn't Christmas without these sweet treats! Fill a Cookie Bucket with Oatmeal Coconut Chocolate Chip Cookies and pass out the Marshmallow Popcorn Balls inside clear Ball Ornaments. How jolly!

2 c. brown sugar, packed
2 c. sugar
1 c. shortening
³/₄ c. butter, softened
4 eggs
2 t. vanilla extract
3 c. all-purpose flour
2 t. salt
2 t. baking soda
3 c. long-cooking oats
2 c. sweetened flaked coconut
1 c. semi-sweet chocolate chips
1 c. chopped pecans

Beat sugars, shortening and butter with an electric mixer until fluffy. Add eggs and vanilla; beat until combined. Combine flour, salt and baking soda; add to sugar mixture, blending well. Stir in remaining ingredients.

Drop dough by 2 tablespoonfuls onto parchment-lined baking sheets. Bake at 350 degrees for 12 to 14 minutes. Let cool 3 minutes on baking sheets; remove cookies to wire racks to cool completely. Makes 6¹/₂ dozen.

Oatmeal Coconut Chocolate Chip Cookies
Cookie Bucket

Cookie Bucket

- green metal pail (ours is 4³/₄"h with a 5³/₄" dia. opening)
- sandpaper
- patterned and solid cardstock
- double-sided tape
- red ribbons and jute twine
- craft glue
- adhesive foam dots
- tag sticker
- patterned food tissue paper
- Oatmeal Coconut Chocolate Chip Cookies

1. Lightly sand the pail to give it an aged appearance.
2. Enlarge the patterns (page 144) to 200%. Use the enlarged patterns to cut the ornament pieces from cardstock.
3. Tape ribbon to the top piece; then, tape the ornament pieces and cap together. Glue a twine loop "hanger" to the back and attach the ornament to the pail with foam dots.
4. Write a message on a cardstock-backed tag sticker. Fill the pail with cookies nestled in tissue paper.

cookies for you!

Marshmallow Popcorn Balls
Ball Ornaments

Marshmallow Popcorn Balls
Kids will love to help make these colorful Christmas treats.

26 c. popped popcorn
1¼ c. dry-roasted salted peanuts
½ c. fruit-flavored gumdrops
½ c. butter
¼ c. canola oil
9 c. mini marshmallows

In a large bowl, combine popcorn, peanuts and gumdrops; toss well. Over low heat, melt together butter, oil and marshmallows; stir until melted. Pour over popcorn mixture to coat. Shape mixture into 16 balls, about 1½ cups each. Makes about 16 balls.

Ball Ornament
- plastic-wrapped Marshmallow Popcorn Ball
- 4" dia. clear acrylic separating ball ornament
- solid and patterned cardstock
- craft glue
- 1¼" smooth and 1½" scalloped circle punches
- black fine-point permanent pen
- loopy ribbon trims for flowers
- corsage pin
- 2 shank buttons
- ribbons
- hole punch

1. Place a popcorn ball in the ornament.
2. Trim 2 corners from a 2¼"x4" cardstock tag. Layer and glue smooth and scalloped cardstock circles on the tag; add a holiday message.
3. Coil a trim piece into a large round flower on the tag, gluing as you go. Insert the pin in the flower and glue a button to the center.
4. Glue a small trim flower and button to the tag. Loop ribbons through a hole punched in the tag and hang from the ornament.

77

Holiday Open House

One of the best things about Christmas is the chance to celebrate the spirit of the season with family & friends! This collection of finger foods and desserts offers something delicious for every taste. From Crispy Chicken Fingers to Cheesecake Cranberry Bars, you'll find everything you need for hosting a casual open house gathering...and most of these recipes can be prepared ahead of time!

Crispy Chicken Fingers

Look for frozen chicken strips for an even speedier appetizer!

4 boneless, skinless chicken
    breasts
1 c. all-purpose flour
1 t. salt
¼ t. pepper
¾ c. milk
vegetable oil

Cut chicken into 2½-inch strips; set aside. Combine flour, salt and pepper in a large plastic zipping bag; set aside.

Dip chicken strips in milk. Place chicken in flour mixture; seal bag and shake to coat. Fry coated chicken strips in 350-degree deep oil for 3 minutes on each side or until golden. Place on paper towels to drain. Serve with Honey-Mustard Sauce. Makes about 2 dozen.

Honey-Mustard Sauce:
½ c. honey
¼ c. Dijon mustard
2 T. yellow mustard

Combine ingredients and mix well. Keep refrigerated up to one or 2 days. Makes one cup.

Vickie

Crispy Chicken Fingers

Ham & Swiss Rolls

Ham & Swiss Rolls

Be sure to buy dinner rolls that come in foil pans.

¼ c. Dijon mustard
1 onion, minced
1 c. butter, melted
4 oz. Swiss cheese, grated
2 T. poppy seed
1 T. Worcestershire sauce
1 lb. shaved deli ham
4 pkgs. small dinner rolls

Combine mustard, onion, butter, cheese, poppy seed and Worcestershire sauce in a small bowl. Using a serrated knife, slice an entire package of rolls in half, horizontally. Spread the bottom half with ¼ of the mustard mixture, top with ¼ lb. ham and replace the top half. Repeat with remaining rolls, mustard mixture, and ham. Return rolls to foil pans. Bake at 325 degrees for 20 to 30 minutes, or until thoroughly heated.

Charmaine Hahl

Easy Sweet-and-Sour Meatballs

A quick and easy appetizer for guests and potlucks...keep it warm by serving right from the slow cooker.

2-lb. pkg. frozen meatballs, thawed
2 8-oz cans pineapple tidbits
18-oz. bottle barbecue sauce
1 onion, diced
1 green pepper, diced
Optional: ¼ c. chopped fresh parsley

Combine all ingredients except parsley in a 4-quart slow cooker. Cover and cook on low setting 2 hours or until heated through. Stir in parsley just before serving, if desired.

Lynn Fazz
Yuma, AZ

Easy Sweet-and-Sour Meatballs

Zesty Corn Salsa
Spicy Guacamole

You can feed a crowd in a hurry with hearty Ham & Swiss Rolls and Easy Sweet-and-Sour Meatballs. Turn your get-together into a real fiesta by setting out generous dishes of Zesty Corn Salsa and Spicy Guacamole!

Zesty Corn Salsa

This simple salsa is even better when made the day before.

2 c. frozen corn, thawed
1/4 c. red pepper, chopped
2 green onions, sliced
1 jalapeño pepper, seeded and chopped
1 T. fresh cilantro, chopped
2 T. lime juice
1 T. oil
1/2 t. salt
corn chips

Gently stir together first 8 ingredients; cover and refrigerate at least one hour before serving. Serve with corn chips. Makes 2 1/2 cups.

Connie Fortune
Covington, OH

Spicy Guacamole

Serve this festive dip with your favorite tortilla chips and veggies.

4 avocados, pitted, peeled and chopped
1 clove garlic, minced
2 T. lemon juice
1 t. pepper
1 tomato, diced
1/2 t. salt
1/8 t. cayenne pepper

Mash avocados with a fork; stir in remaining ingredients. Makes about 2 cups.

Sharon Reagan
Concord, NH

Loaded Potato Rounds

An amazing combination of flavors…you'll love these!

2 baking potatoes
olive oil
1 c. shredded Colby Jack cheese
6 slices bacon, crisply cooked and crumbled
1/3 c. green onion, sliced
1/4 c. barbecue sauce

Cut unpeeled potatoes into 1/4-inch-thick rounds. Brush both sides with oil; arrange in one layer on an ungreased baking sheet. Bake at 450 degrees for 20 minutes, or until tender and golden.

Combine cheese, bacon and onion in a small bowl; set aside. Brush baked potato rounds with barbecue sauce; sprinkle with cheese mixture. Bake an additional 3 to 5 minutes, or until cheese is melted. Makes 2 1/2 dozen.

Claudine King
Fremont, MI

Fill the air with the heavenly smell of Holiday Wassail! The fruit-and-cinnamon drink will warm everyone's heart with a classic flavor of Christmas. Cranberry sauce is another great taste of the season, and it's especially welcome when baked into Cheesecake Cranberry Bars.

Artichoke-Cheese Squares

You can make these ahead and freeze until you need them. Enjoy hot or cold.

2 6-oz. jars artichoke hearts
1/2 red onion, finely chopped
1/4 c. dry bread crumbs
1/8 t. pepper
1/8 t. dried oregano
1/8 t. hot pepper sauce
1 1/2 c. grated Cheddar cheese
1/2 c. grated Parmesan cheese
2 T. fresh parsley, chopped
4 eggs, beaten

Drain artichokes, reserving liquid from jar. Slice artichokes; set aside.

Sauté onion in artichoke liquid for about 3 minutes or until tender. Combine bread crumbs and remaining ingredients in a large bowl. Stir in artichokes and onion mixture. Pour into a greased 13"x9" baking pan. Bake at 325 degrees for 30 minutes. Let cool in dish 15 minutes; cut into squares.

★ tree trio ★

82

Holiday Wassail

We have had this recipe in our family for years. The sweet aromas of nutmeg and cinnamon will fill the house with holiday cheer.

64-oz. can apple juice
64-oz. can pineapple juice
1/3 c. lemon juice
1/4 c. honey
1/4 t. nutmeg
4-inch cinnamon stick
Garnishes: lemon slices and cinnamon sticks, optional

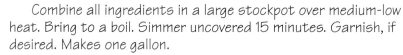

Combine all ingredients in a large stockpot over medium-low heat. Bring to a boil. Simmer uncovered 15 minutes. Garnish, if desired. Makes one gallon.

Lori Downing
Bradenton, FL

Holiday Wassail

Cheesecake Cranberry Bars

Cheesecake Cranberry Bars
These pebbly-topped holiday bars will disappear in a flash.

2 c. all-purpose flour
1 1/2 c. long-cooking oats, uncooked
1/4 c. brown sugar, packed
1 c. butter, softened
12-oz. pkg. white chocolate chips
8-oz. pkg. cream cheese, softened
14-oz. can sweetened condensed milk
1/4 c. lemon juice
1 t. vanilla extract
14-oz. can whole-berry cranberry sauce
2 T. cornstarch

In a large bowl, combine flour, oats and brown sugar; cut in butter until coarse crumbs form. Stir in chocolate chips; reserve 2 1/2 cups of crumb mixture for topping. With floured fingers, press remaining mixture into a greased 13"x9" baking pan; set aside. Beat cream cheese in a large bowl until creamy. Add condensed milk, lemon juice and vanilla; mix until smooth. Pour cream cheese mixture over crust. Combine cranberry sauce and cornstarch; spoon over cream cheese mixture. Sprinkle reserved crumb mixture over top. Bake at 375 degrees for 35 to 40 minutes, or until golden. Let cool and cut into bars. Makes 2 dozen.

Linda Galvin
Ames, IA

Chocolate Fondue
A fun dessert the whole family will love. Experiment with your favorite candy bars for a new twist.

2 8-oz. chocolate candy bars with almonds
2 to 4 T. light cream
Optional: 1 t. cherry brandy or peppermint liqueur
Items for dipping: marshmallows, bananas and pineapple, maraschino cherries, pound cake, shortbread cookies

Melt chocolate over low heat. Add cream. Cook, stirring constantly, about 5 minutes or until thickened. Stir in liqueur, if using. To serve, spoon into a fondue pot and keep warm over heat source.

Echo Renner
Meeteetse, WY

CHRISTMAS DINNER ♥ Classics

These are the dishes we remember from years gone by! Each one is full of old-fashioned flavor. Roast your turkey with savory butter, serve up a yummy Sweet Onion Casserole and bake melt-in-your mouth Popovers. From Rosemary Pork Roast with Tangerine-Cranberry Relish to Maple-Pecan Pie, these recipes were sent to the Country Friends from good cooks all over the country. See how many delicious memories you can find in these pages. Christmas dinner should always taste this good!

Roast Turkey with Sage Butter

An All-American dish that's perfect for your holiday table.

1 c. butter, softened
3 T. fresh sage, chopped
8 slices bacon, crisply cooked
    and crumbled
salt and pepper to taste
16-lb. turkey, thawed if frozen
3 c. leeks, chopped
8 sprigs fresh sage
3 bay leaves, crumbled
4 c. chicken broth, divided
Garnishes: fresh sage sprigs,
    parsley sprigs, fresh cherries,
    plums and grapes

Combine butter, sage and bacon; sprinkle with salt and pepper. Set aside.

Remove giblets and neck from turkey; reserve for another use. Rinse turkey and pat dry. Sprinkle inside of turkey with salt and pepper; add leeks, sage and bay leaves. Loosen skin and spread 1/3 cup butter mixture over breast meat under skin. Place turkey on rack of a large broiler pan. Rub 2 tablespoons butter mixture over turkey. Set aside 1/3 cup mixture for gravy; reserve remainder for basting. Pour 1/3 cup broth over turkey.

Bake turkey at 350 degrees for about 2 1/2 hours, or until a meat thermometer inserted into thickest part of inner thigh registers 170 degrees, shielding to prevent overbrowning. Baste every 30 minutes with 1/3 cup broth; brush occasionally with remaining butter mixture. Transfer turkey to a platter; keep warm.

For gravy, pour juices and bits from pan into large measuring cup. Spoon off fat and discard. Bring juices and 2 cups broth to a boil in a large saucepan; boil until liquid is reduced to 2 cups, about 6 minutes. Whisk in reserved 1/3 cup butter mixture. Season with pepper. Garnish, if desired. Serve turkey with gravy. Serves 12.

Kendall Hale
Lynn, MA

Roast Turkey with Sage Butter

85

Rosemary Pork Roast with Tangerine-Cranberry Relish

Arrange pork slices over mashed potatoes for a farm-style meal that's so hearty and filling.

3 cloves garlic, minced
1 T. dried rosemary
salt and pepper to taste
2-lb. boneless pork loin roast
2 T. olive oil
1/2 c. white wine or chicken broth

Tangerine-Cranberry Relish:
1 lb. cranberries
4 tangerines
2 c. seedless raisins or nuts, coarsely chopped
1 1/2 to 2 c. sugar

Crush garlic with rosemary, salt and pepper. Pierce pork with a sharp knife tip in several places and press half the garlic mixture into openings. Rub pork with remaining garlic mixture and olive oil. Place pork in a lightly greased 13"x9" baking pan.

Bake, uncovered, at 350 degrees for 1 hour and 15 minutes or until a meat thermometer inserted into thickest portion registers 155 degrees. Let stand, covered, 10 minutes or until thermometer registers 160 degrees. Remove to a serving platter; slice and keep warm. Add wine or broth to pan, stirring to loosen browned bits. Spoon pan drippings over pork and serve with Tangerine-Cranberry Relish. Serves 8.

Tiffany Brinkley
Broomfield, CO

Wash cranberries (do not thaw berries if frozen) and put into a food processor; pulse until chopped. Set aside.

Wash tangerines and remove peel. Put the peel into food processor; pulse until finely chopped.

Remove seeds from tangerines and cut sections into smaller pieces. Combine cranberries, tangerine peel and pieces and sugar in a medium saucepan; add raisins or nuts. Add sugar and cook 15 minutes over medium heat, stirring occasionally until thickened. Serve warm or pour into jelly glasses. Relish may be stored in refrigerator for 2 to 4 weeks. Makes 2 1/2 pints.

Rosemary Pork Roast with Tangerine-Cranberry Relish

Sweet & zingy Tangerine-Cranberry Relish is the perfect complement to Rosemary Pork Roast. A Southern favorite, Cornbread Stuffing with Sage & Sausage is a hearty side dish your family will love.

Caramelized Brussels Sprouts

These go great with a golden turkey and all the trimmings. My friend Lisa and I usually eat any leftovers before we can put them away!

4 lbs. Brussels sprouts, halved
1/2 c. butter
4 onions, halved and thinly sliced
1/4 c. red wine vinegar, divided
2 T. sugar
salt and pepper to taste
Optional: 1/2 c. pistachio nuts, chopped

Place Brussels sprouts and 2" water in a Dutch oven; bring to a boil. Cover and steam 8 to 10 minutes, or until just crisp-tender.

Meanwhile, melt butter in a large skillet. Add onions and 3 tablespoons vinegar; cook until golden. Add Brussels sprouts, sugar and remaining vinegar. Sauté over medium heat until Brussels sprouts are lightly caramelized. Sprinkle with salt, pepper and nuts, if desired. Serves 8.

Beth Schlieper
Lakewood, CO

Sweet Onion Casserole

5 sweet onions, sliced into thin rings
1 c. butter, softened
24 round buttery crackers, crushed
1/2 c. grated Parmesan cheese
Optional: 2 T. milk

Sauté onions in melted butter in a skillet over medium heat, 15 minutes or until tender. Spoon half of onions into a 1 1/2 quart baking dish. Sprinkle half of cracker crumbs and half of cheese over onions; repeat layers. Bake, uncovered, at 325 degrees for 25 to 30 minutes. Add milk if crackers have absorbed too much liquid. Serves 6 to 8.

Virginia King-Hugill
Woodinville, WA

Cornbread Stuffing with Sage & Sausage

Cornbread Stuffing with Sage & Sausage

Use mild sausage and thyme, if you prefer.

8" square day-old cornbread, cut into 1/2-inch cubes
1 lb. sweet Italian ground pork sausage
2 small onions, finely chopped
6 stalks celery, finely chopped
2 cloves garlic, minced
1 T. dried sage
Optional: 1/2 c. pine nuts, toasted
1 c. chicken broth
1/4 c. butter, melted
salt and pepper to taste

Spread cornbread evenly on a baking sheet. Bake at 350 degrees for 20 minutes, or until golden brown.

Brown sausage in a large skillet over medium-high heat; drain, reserving one teaspoon of drippings in pan. Add onion, celery and garlic to drippings in pan. Sauté over medium heat until tender.

Combine sausage, onion mixture, cornbread, sage and pine nuts, if desired, in a large bowl and mix well. Add chicken broth and melted butter and toss to combine. Season with salt and pepper to taste. Transfer to a greased 13"x9" baking dish. Bake, uncovered, at 350 degrees for 1 hour or until golden. Makes 8 to 10 servings.

87

Praline-Topped Butternut Squash

When we're invited to a family gathering I'm always asked to bring this dish.

3 12-oz. pkgs. frozen butternut
　　squash purée
7 T. butter, divided
1/2 t. salt
1/8 t. pepper
2 eggs, beaten
1/2 t. cinnamon
1/2 c. brown sugar, packed
1/8 t. nutmeg
1/2 c. chopped pecans

Praline-Topped Butternut Squash

Heat squash according to microwave package directions; stir in 1/4 cup butter, salt and pepper. Add eggs, mixing well. Spoon mixture into a greased one-quart baking dish; set aside.

Combine cinnamon, brown sugar, remaining butter, nutmeg and pecans; sprinkle over squash mixture. Bake, uncovered, at 350 degrees for 30 minutes. Serves 8.

Nancy Kowalski
Southbury, CT

Herb Seasoned Beans

These are also great in the summer when you can find fresh green beans at the farmer's market.

1 c. water
8 c. fresh green beans, trimmed
1/2 c. butter, melted
1/2 c. seasoned bread crumbs
4 t. fresh parsley, chopped

In a Dutch oven, cover green beans with water. Simmer 15 minutes or until crisp-tender; drain.

Combine butter and remaining ingredients. Add green beans, mixing well. Serves 10.

Debbie Cummons-Parker
Lakeview, OH

Crunchy Salad Almondine
Very pretty for a special holiday luncheon or buffet table!

1/4 c. butter
1/2 c. slivered almonds
1 head lettuce, chopped
2 c. celery, chopped
2 T. fresh parsley, chopped
2 c. green onions, chopped
2 11-oz. cans mandarin oranges,
　　drained
1/2 c. oil
1/2 t. hot pepper sauce
1/4 c. sugar
1 t. salt
1/8 t. pepper
1/4 c. tarragon vinegar

Melt butter in a small skillet. Add almonds and sauté 2 minutes or until toasted; set aside to cool.

In a large serving bowl, combine lettuce, celery, parsley, green onions, mandarin oranges and almonds; refrigerate until ready to serve.

Whisk together oil, hot pepper sauce, sugar, salt, pepper and tarragon vinegar, until thoroughly mixed. Pour dressing over salad just before serving.

Jackie Crough
Salina, KS

Don't forget the veggies, especially when they're so wonderful! Enjoying Praline-Topped Butternut Squash is almost like eating dessert right along with the main course. With raisins, walnuts, bacon and cabbage in the mix, Cranberry Broccoli Salad offers a world of flavor in every bite.

Old-Fashioned Yeast Rolls

2 pkgs. active dry yeast
1/3 c. warm water
1 c. butter
1 1/2 c. milk
4 1/2 to 5 c. all-purpose flour
1/2 c. sugar
1 t. salt
2 eggs, beaten

Combine yeast and warm water (110 to 115 degrees); let stand 5 minutes.

Combine butter and milk in a small saucepan; cook over low heat until melted. Let stand until mixture reaches a temperature between 110 and 115 degrees. Add yeast mixture and stir until blended.

Meanwhile, combine 4 1/2 cups flour, sugar and salt in a large mixing bowl. Add milk mixture and eggs; beat at medium speed with an electric mixer until well blended.

Turn dough out onto a floured surface, and knead in enough of remaining flour to make a soft dough. Knead until smooth and elastic (about 10 minutes). Place in a well-greased bowl, turning to grease top.

Cover dough with plastic wrap, and let rise in a warm place (85 degrees), free from drafts, until dough doubles in bulk.

Punch dough down; turn out onto a lightly floured surface and knead lightly 4 or 5 times. Shape into rolls and arrange in a buttered and floured 13"X9" baking pan. Cover and let dough double in bulk. Bake at 400 degrees for 15 to 20 minutes or until golden. Makes 3 dozen.

Cranberry Broccoli Salad
Old-Fashioned Yeast Rolls

Cranberry Broccoli Salad
Colorful, crunchy and refreshing.

1 1/4 c. cranberries, halved
2 c. broccoli flowerets
4 c. cabbage, shredded
1 c. walnuts, coarsely chopped
1/2 c. raisins
1 small onion, finely chopped
8 slices bacon, crisply cooked and crumbled
1 c. mayonnaise
1/3 c. sugar
2 T. cider vinegar

Combine first 7 ingredients; toss well. Combine remaining ingredients, stirring well with a whisk. Drizzle mayonnaise mixture over cranberry mixture and toss to coat. Cover and refrigerate for up to 24 hours. Makes 6 to 8 servings.

Popovers

Mom's beef stew wasn't complete without a batch of popovers straight from the oven. As kids we'd peel the tops off and use them to sop up the leftover stew in the bottom of our bowls. We'd butter the bottom and eat them while the steam was still escaping.

1 c. milk
1 T. butter, melted
1 c. all-purpose flour
¹/₄ t. salt
2 eggs

Let all ingredients come to room temperature. Stir together milk, butter, flour and salt in a large mixing bowl. Add eggs, one at a time, beating until blended; do not over beat.

Pour batter into large buttered muffin pans, filling ³/₄ full. Bake at 450 degrees for 15 minutes. Reduce heat to 350 degrees and bake 20 more minutes or until edges of rolls are firm.

Kara Allison
Dublin, OH

Popovers

Old-fashioned Popovers are so easy to make, you'll wonder why you don't serve them all the time. Add a spoonful of thick whipped cream to your piece of the Maple-Pecan Pie, or go for the rich custard in the heavenly Tiramisu. Surely homemade treats can't get better than this!

Maple-Pecan Pie

Great anytime, but seems to be just about perfect when served warm on a chilly day.

4 eggs, lightly beaten
²/₃ c. sugar
¹/₂ t. salt
6 T. butter, melted
1 c. maple syrup
1¹/₂ c. pecan halves
9-inch unbaked pie crust
Garnish: whipped topping

Combine first 5 ingredients in a large bowl; stir well with a wire whisk until blended. Sprinkle pecan halves into pie crust; pour syrup mixture over pecans. Bake at 375 degrees for 15 minutes; lower oven temperature to 350 degrees and bake 25 more minutes or until center is set. Cover with aluminum foil after 25 minutes to prevent excessive browning, if necessary. Cool completely on a wire rack. Serve with whipped topping, if desired. Makes 8 servings.

Peggy Bowman
Palisade, CO

Tiramisu

Maple Pecan Pie

Tiramisu

No wonder this fabulous dessert is popular in many Italian restaurants!

3/4 c. sugar
2 c. milk, divided
6 egg yolks
1/4 c. all-purpose flour
4 T. unsalted butter, cut into pieces
1/4 c. light rum
2 t. pure vanilla extract
3/4 c. mascarpone cheese
3 3-oz. pkgs. soft ladyfingers
2 c. espresso or very strong, freshly
    brewed coffee
Garnish: whipped cream, cocoa and
    chocolate curls

In a heavy saucepan over medium heat, combine sugar and all but 2 tablespoons of milk. Cook just until boiling and until sugar dissolves completely.

In a bowl, beat the egg yolks with reserved 2 tablespoons of milk and flour. Gradually add hot milk mixture to the egg mixture, stirring constantly with a wire whisk. Return mixture to saucepan. Cook over medium heat until mixture comes to a boil, whisking constantly. Boil 2 minutes or until thickened. Remove from the heat and strain into a clean bowl. Whisk in the butter, rum and vanilla. Cover the surface of custard with plastic wrap; refrigerate 2 hours or until completely cooled.

Place mascarpone cheese into a medium bowl, stirring to soften. Gradually fold in the cooled custard. Brush ladyfingers with espresso. Arrange 1/3 of ladyfingers on the bottom and sides of a trifle dish. Top with 1/3 of custard. Repeat layers twice. Refrigerate for at least one hour. Garnish with whipped cream, sifted cocoa and chocolate curls, if desired.

Individual Tiramisus:
Prepare recipe up to layering step. Divide mixture among 6 to 8 individual custard cups or small trifle dishes, repeating same layering method as above.

91

Blue Ribbon Cakes

Served with ice cream, topped with fruit, or just enjoyed as-is...cake is a dessert everyone loves! These half-dozen delightful recipes were sent to the Country Friends by good cooks across the nation. Try the Strawberry Cake for a flavor of springtime in December. Or slice into the ooey-gooey, marshmallow goodness of Mississippi Mud Layer Cake. Know someone who's nutty for bananas? Surprise them with a Banana-Walnut Upside Down Cake!

Raspberry Truffle Cheesecake

Garnish with whipped cream, raspberries and mint leaves for a beautiful presentation.

1½ c. chocolate sandwich cookies, crushed (about 18 cookies)
2 T. butter, melted
4 8-oz. pkgs. cream cheese, softened, divided
1¼ c. sugar
3 eggs
1 c. sour cream
1 t. almond extract
2 6-oz. pkgs. chocolate chips
⅓ c. seedless raspberry jam
¼ c. whipping cream

In a small bowl, mix together cookies and butter. Press into bottom of a 9" springform pan; set aside.

In a mixing bowl, beat 3 packages of cream cheese and sugar at medium speed with an electric mixer until smooth. Add eggs, one at a time, beating at low speed just until combined. Add sour cream and almond extract; beat just until blended. Pour over crust; set aside.

Place one package of chocolate chips in a medium microwave-safe bowl; microwave 30 seconds to one minute or until melted. Add remaining package of cream cheese and jam to melted chocolate; blend until smooth. Drop chocolate mixture by rounded tablespoonfuls onto batter in pan; do not swirl. Bake at 325 degrees for one hour and 20 minutes. Remove from oven and run knife around sides of pan to remove sides. Cool completely in pan on a wire rack. Remove from pan and place on a serving platter or cake plate.

In a medium saucepan, heat remaining chocolate chips and whipping cream over low heat; stir until smooth. Spread over cheesecake. Cover and chill 8 hours. Serves 12 to 14.

Deborah Hilton
Oswego, NY

Raspberry Truffle Cheesecake

Double-Coconut Cake

A snowy white cake that is just as delicious as it is pretty.

2¼ c. cake flour
2¼ t. baking powder
½ t. salt
1⅔ c. sugar
⅓ c. butter, softened
2 eggs
1 T. vanilla extract
14-oz. can coconut milk
⅔ c. sweetened flaked coconut, divided

Stir together first 3 ingredients in a medium bowl. Beat sugar and butter at medium speed with an electric mixer until fluffy. Add eggs, one at a time, beating after each addition. Stir in vanilla.

Add coconut milk alternately with flour mixture, beginning and ending with flour mixture. Pour batter into 2 greased and floured 9" round cake pans; bake at 350 degrees for 30 minutes or until a toothpick inserted in center comes out clean. Cool in pans on a wire rack for 10 minutes; remove from pans. Cool completely on wire racks.

Spread one cup Fluffy Coconut Frosting in between layers; sprinkle with ⅓ cup coconut. Spread remaining frosting on top and sides of cake. Sprinkle with remaining coconut; refrigerate until chilled. Serves 14.

Fluffy Coconut Frosting:
4 egg whites
½ t. cream of tartar
⅛ t. salt
½ t. vanilla extract
¼ t. coconut extract
1 c. sugar
¼ c. water

Beat egg whites, cream of tartar, salt and extracts at high speed with an electric mixer until soft peaks form. Set aside. Combine sugar and water in a saucepan. Stir to dissolve sugar, then bring to a boil. Continue to boil, without stirring, until mixture reaches the soft-ball stage, or 234 to 243 degrees on a candy thermometer. Remove from heat and pour in a thin stream over egg white mixture. Blend until fluffy. Makes 5 cups.

Debby Phillips
Lamar, IN

Double-Coconut Cake

Strawberry Cake

Be gentle with the frosting so that it doesn't become too runny.

18¼-oz. pkg. white cake mix
3-oz. pkg. strawberry gelatin mix
4 eggs
¾ c. oil
½ c. frozen strawberries, thawed
    and undrained
½ c. water

Combine all ingredients in a large mixing bowl. Beat at medium speed with an electric mixer until well blended. Pour into a greased and floured 13"x9" baking pan and bake at 350 degrees for 33 to 35 minutes; cool. Spread Frosting over cooled cake. Makes 12 to 15 servings.

Frosting:
¼ c. butter, softened
½ c. fresh strawberries, chopped,
    divided
16-oz. pkg. powdered sugar,
    divided

Beat butter at medium speed with an electric mixer until light and fluffy. Add ¼ cup strawberries and about ⅓ of sugar, beating until blended. Gradually add remaining sugar, beating until creamy. Fold in remaining ¼ cup strawberries. Makes 2½ cups.

Melanie Wallace
Corinth, TX

Strawberry Cake

Made from scratch, the Double-Coconut Cake gets rich flavor from coconut milk. Use a cake mix and strawberry gelatin to save time when you bake a Strawberry Cake.

Sweet Potato Pound Cake

This old-fashioned dessert will scent your kitchen with the aroma of cinnamon and spice as it bakes.

1 c. butter, softened
1½ c. sugar
¼ c. brown sugar, packed
2½ c. sweet potatoes, peeled,
    cooked and mashed
4 eggs
1 T. vanilla extract
3 c. all-purpose flour
2 t. baking powder
1 t. baking soda
1 t. salt
1½ t. cinnamon
¼ t. nutmeg
¼ t. mace

In a bowl, beat butter and sugars until fluffy. Add sweet potatoes; beat thoroughly. Add eggs, one at a time, beating well after each addition; stir in vanilla. Whisk together remaining ingredients. Gradually add to butter mixture, beating at low speed until blended. Pour batter into a lightly greased and floured 10" tube pan. Bake at 350 degrees for one hour, or until cake tests done. Serves 10 to 12.

Cindy Spears
Keithville, LA

Mississippi Mud Layer Cake

(shown on front cover)
Ooey-gooey Mississippi Mud Cake is transformed into a festive Christmas layer cake. Use your favorite Christmas sprinkles or large marshmallows, if desired.

1¹/₂ c. butter
³/₄ c. cocoa
6 eggs, beaten
3 c. sugar
2 c. all-purpose flour
¹/₄ t. salt
1 t. vanilla extract
3 c. mini marshmallows
Garnish: mini marshmallows, melted white chocolate, red and green sprinkles

Melt butter and cocoa over low heat; cool. Add eggs and sugar, mixing well. Stir in flour, salt and vanilla. Pour batter into three 8" round cake pans and bake at 325 degrees for 25 minutes or until a toothpick inserted in center comes out clean with a few crumbs attached. Remove from oven and sprinkle each layer with 1 cup marshmallows. Return to oven and bake 2 more minutes or until marshmallows begin to puff. Let cool in pans on wire racks 10 minutes. Remove from pans and cool completely. Spread Chocolate Frosting between layers and on top and sides of cake. Garnish, if desired.

Chocolate Frosting:
1 c. butter, softened
²/₃ c. cocoa
2 16-oz. pkgs. powdered sugar
¹/₃ c. milk

Beat butter with an electric mixer until fluffy. Gradually add cocoa and powdered sugar, beating until blended. Add milk, beating until desired spreading consistency.

Gail Goudy
Walls, MS

Not a pineapple in sight…it's the sweet flavor of bananas and the crunch of walnuts in maple syrup that make Banana-Walnut Upside Down Cake so special. So indulgent!

Banana-Walnut Upside Down Cake

Here's a twist on an old-time favorite that was popular in the 1950s.

1 c. brown sugar, packed
¹/₂ c. plus 2 T. butter, divided
3 T. pure maple syrup
¹/₄ c. walnuts, coarsely chopped and toasted
4 ripe bananas, peeled and sliced
³/₄ c. sugar
1 egg
¹/₂ t. vanilla extract
1 c. all-purpose flour
2 t. baking powder
¹/₂ t. cinnamon
¹/₄ t. salt
6 T. milk
Garnish: sweetened whipped cream

Combine brown sugar and ¹/₄ cup butter in a saucepan; cook over low heat until butter melts and mixture is well blended. Pour in a 9" round cake pan, spreading to coat bottom of pan. Pour maple syrup over sugar mixture and sprinkle evenly with walnuts. Place banana slices in concentric circles over nuts, overlapping slightly and covering bottom.

Blend together sugar and remaining 6 tablespoons butter until fluffy in a large mixing bowl; add egg and vanilla, beating until well blended. Combine flour, baking powder, cinnamon and salt; gradually add to creamed mixture alternately with milk, beginning and ending with flour mixture. Spoon batter over bananas and bake at 325 degrees for 55 minutes or until a toothpick inserted in center comes out clean. Carefully run a knife around the edge of pan to loosen. Cool in pan on a wire rack 30 minutes; invert cake onto a serving platter. Let stand 3 minutes; remove cake from pan. Serve warm with whipped cream.

Judy Clark
Jacksonville, FL

Always bear in mind that your own resolution to success is more important than any other one thing.
—ABRAHAM LINCOLN—

Banana-Walnut Upside Down Cake

The Yummy Comfort of Casseroles

When you need to feed a hungry household on a cold day, a warm casserole is hard to beat! Treat your family and holiday guests to individual dishes of Golden Chicken Divan. Fluffy potatoes with parmesan top a mix of savory beef and veggies in Momma's Shepherd's Pie. Cheesy Baked Spaghetti serves a crowd…or a family of pasta lovers who want seconds!

Golden Chicken Divan

This casserole is always a crowd-pleaser.

1 lb. broccoli, chopped
1½ c. cooked chicken, cubed
10¾ oz. can cream of chicken soup
⅓ c. sour cream
½ t. garlic powder
½ t. curry powder
½ t. onion powder
¼ t. seasoned salt
½ c. shredded Cheddar cheese
1 T. butter, melted
¼ c. round buttery crackers, crushed

Cover broccoli with water in a saucepan; bring to a boil over medium heat. Cook 5 minutes or until tender; drain. In a large bowl, combine broccoli, chicken, soup, sour cream, garlic power, curry powder, onion powder and salt. Spread in a greased 8"x8" baking dish; sprinkle with cheese. Mix together melted butter and crackers; sprinkle over cheese. Bake, uncovered, at 450 degrees for 10 minutes or until bubbly and golden. Serves 6.

Amy Kim
Ann Arbor, MI

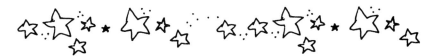

Golden Chicken Divan

Sausage & Chicken Cassoulet

This traditional French casserole is full of wonderful flavors.
Serve it with some hearty bread to sop up the tasty juices.

1 lb. ground hot Italian pork sausage
1 c. carrots, peeled and thinly sliced
1 onion, diced
2 t. garlic, minced
1 c. red wine or beef broth
1 T. tomato paste
1 bay leaf
1 t. fresh thyme leaves
1 t. chopped fresh rosemary
salt and pepper to taste
2 c. cooked chicken, diced
2 15-oz. cans Great Northern beans, undrained
Garnishes: fresh thyme leaves and chopped fresh rosemary

Brown sausage in an oven-safe Dutch oven; drain. Add carrots, onion and garlic. Sauté for 3 minutes; drain. Add wine or broth, tomato paste, bay leaf, thyme, rosemary, salt and pepper; bring to a boil. Remove pan from heat; stir in chicken and beans. Bake, covered, at 350 degrees for 45 minutes or until bubbly. Discard bay leaf before serving. Garnish with fresh herbs, if desired. Serves 4 to 6.

Diane Stout
Zeeland, MI

If your gang likes to work up an appetite playing in the great outdoors, fill them up with hearty Sausage & Chicken Cassoulet. Need a quick meal? Momma's Shepherd's Pie is simple to make, leaving you more time to wrap gifts or trim the tree!

Chicken & Wild Rice Casserole

The ultimate comfort food casserole! Try with leftover turkey too, when you have Thanksgiving leftovers and houseguests to feed.

1/4 c. butter
1 onion, chopped
4 stalks celery, chopped
8-oz. can sliced water chestnuts, drained
2 6-oz. pkgs. long-grain and wild rice, cooked
5 c. cooked chicken, chopped
16-oz. pkg, shredded Cheddar cheese, divided
2 10³/4 oz. cans cream of mushroom soup
16-oz. container sour cream
1 c. milk
1/2 t. salt
1/2 c. bread crumbs

In a large skillet, melt butter over medium heat. Add onion, celery and water chestnuts; sauté 10 minutes, or until tender. Stir in rice, chicken, 3 cups cheese, soup, sour cream, milk and salt. Spread in a lightly greased 13"x9" baking pan; sprinkle with bread crumbs. Bake, uncovered, at 350 degrees for 30 minutes. Sprinkle with remaining cheese and bake for an additional 5 minutes. Serves 8.

Karen Lehmann
New Braunfels, TX

Sausage & Chicken Cassoulet

Momma's Shepherd's Pie

Lee's Trim-The-Tree Turkey Tetrazzini

This heart-warming casserole can be made ahead and refrigerated. Just be sure to let it stand 1 hour at room temperature before baking.

1/2 c. butter, divided
1/4 c. all-purpose flour
1 c. evaporated milk
1 c. milk
2 c. turkey or chicken stock
1/3 c. dry sherry
3 4 oz. cans mushrooms, drained
1 t. oil
1 lb. thin spaghetti (broken into 3" to 4" pieces), cooked
4 c. cooked turkey, cubed
1 c. grated Cheddar cheese
1/2 c. bread crumbs

In a large skillet, melt 1/4 cup butter over medium heat. Stir in flour. Add evaporated milk, chicken broth and whole milk; cook, stirring constantly, until sauce is thickened. Remove pan from heat; stir in sherry.

Sauté mushrooms in oil and 1 teaspoon butter in a Dutch oven over medium heat until tender. Fold in cooked spaghetti, cream sauce, and turkey and place in a buttered 4-quart or two 2-quart baking dishes. Combine cheese, bread crumbs and remaining butter; sprinkle cheese mixture over top of noodle mixture. Bake, covered, at 425 degrees for 15 minutes. Uncover and bake 15 to 20 more minutes or until golden and bubbly.

Lee Charrier

Momma's Shepherd's Pie

This recipe is very quick to prepare, looks delicious and tastes even better...my family loves it!

24-oz. pkg. refrigerated mashed potatoes
1 1/2 lbs. ground beef, browned and drained
10 3/4 oz. can cream of mushroom soup
14 1/2 oz. can green beans, drained
15 1/4 oz. can corn, drained
2 eggs, beaten
1/2 c. grated Parmesan cheese
1 1/2 c. shredded sharp Cheddar cheese
1/2 c. Colby cheese, shredded

Cook mashed potatoes according to package directions; set aside.

Stir together ground beef, soup, green beans and corn; spread in an ungreased 11"x7" baking dish. Set aside.

Combine mashed potatoes, eggs and Parmesan cheese; spread over meat mixture. Top with shredded cheeses. Bake, uncovered, at 375 degrees for 45 minutes. Let stand 10 minutes before serving. Serves 4.

Barb Scott
Bowling Green, IN

Mom's Famous Macaroni & Cheese

This recipe is the best macaroni & cheese I have ever eaten! The recipe was given to me by my mother, Bessie Wilson, who has been preparing this dish for 60 years. It is always a must-have for her children, grandchildren and great-grandchildren.

8-oz. pkg. elbow macaroni, cooked
6 T. butter, softened
5-oz. can evaporated milk
1 c. milk
2 eggs, beaten
12-oz. pkg. shredded Cheddar cheese, divided

Combine macaroni, butter, milks, eggs and 2 cups shredded cheese; mix well. Spoon into a greased 13"x9" baking dish; top with remaining cheese. Bake, uncovered, at 350 degrees for 30 minutes or until golden. Makes 8 to 10 servings.

Sonja Wilsey
Alachua, FL

The sweet onions in Paula's Corn Casserole make it a side dish that goes well with just about anything else you want to serve. Everyone knows spaghetti is an inexpensive way to feed a group, but when you add butter and evaporated milk to Cheesy Baked Spaghetti, it becomes extra-special!

Paula's Corn Casserole

Easy Chicken Enchiladas

This family-friendly dish is so simple to put together.

8-oz. can chicken, drained
1 onion, chopped
8-oz. pkg. shredded Monterey
    Jack cheese, divided
2 14-oz. cans enchilada sauce,
    divided
12 6-inch corn tortillas
Garnish: chopped lettuce,
    chopped tomato, sour cream

Combine chicken, onion, one cup cheese and $1/2$ cup sauce in a large bowl; set aside. Spoon enough sauce into a lightly greased 13"x9" baking dish to barely cover bottom; set aside. Spoon remaining sauce into a skillet; heat through. Dip both sides of each tortilla into sauce to soften slightly. Spoon chicken mixture evenly down the center of each tortilla and roll up. Arrange, seam sides down, in baking dish; sprinkle with remaining cheese. Bake, uncovered, at 350 degrees for 20 minutes. Garnish, if desired. Serves 6.

Cindy Shumaker
Grottoes, VA

Paula's Corn Casserole

A must-have side dish for any get-together.

2 sweet onions, thinly sliced
$1/2$ c. butter
8-oz. container sour cream
$1/2$ c. milk
$1/2$ t. dill weed
$1/4$ t. salt
8-oz. pkg. shredded Cheddar
    cheese, divided
1 egg, beaten
$14^3/4$ oz. can creamed corn
$8^1/2$ oz. pkg. cornbread mix
4 drops hot pepper sauce
Garnish: chopped fresh chives
    and additional sour cream

In a large skillet, sauté onions in butter over medium heat until tender.

Combine sour cream, milk, dill weed and salt in a small bowl; stir in one cup cheese. Add onion mixture; set aside.

Combine egg, creamed corn, cornbread mix and pepper sauce in a large bowl. Spread in a greased 3-quart baking dish; spoon onion mixture over top. Sprinkle with remaining cheese. Bake, uncovered, at 350 degrees for 40 to 45 minutes, or until golden. Let stand 10 minutes before serving. Serves 12 to 15.

Paula Marchesi
Lenhartsville, PA

Cheesy Baked Spaghetti

This will easily become a potluck favorite.

16-oz. pkg. spaghetti noodles, cooked
2 24-oz. jars spaghetti sauce
1 lb. ground beef, browned
1 lb. ground Italian pork sausage, browned
¼ c. butter
¼ c. all-purpose flour
¼ c. grated Parmesan cheese
2 t. salt
½ t. garlic powder
12-oz. can evaporated milk
3 c. shredded Italian cheese blend, divided
Garnish: chopped fresh parsley

Combine spaghetti noodles, spaghetti sauce, ground beef and sausage in a large bowl; set aside. Melt butter in a saucepan over medium heat; add flour, Parmesan cheese, salt and garlic powder, stirring constantly until smooth and bubbly. Add evaporated milk and one cup Italian cheese blend; stir until thickened.

Pour half of spaghetti noodle mixture into a greased 13"x9" casserole dish and pour cheese mixture over top. Pour remaining noodle mixture into dish; top with remaining 2 cups Italian cheese blend. Bake, uncovered, at 350 degrees for 25 to 30 minutes. Sprinkle with parsley, if desired. Makes 12 to 18 servings.

Early-Riser Breakfast Casserole

This has become a tradition at Easter and Christmas because it's so easy to prepare the night before and everyone loves it!

8 slices bread, cubed
1 c. shredded Cheddar cheese
1 c. shredded Monterey Jack cheese
1½ lbs. ground pork sausage, browned
4 eggs, beaten
3 c. milk, divided
10¾ oz. can cream of mushroom soup
¾ t. dry mustard

Arrange bread cubes in the bottom of an ungreased 13"X9" baking dish; sprinkle with cheeses and sausage. Set aside.

Beat together eggs and 2½ cups milk; pour over bread. Cover with aluminum foil, refrigerate overnight.

Combine remaining ½ cup milk, cream of mushroom soup and mustard; pour over bread mixture. Bake, uncovered, at 300 degrees for 1½ hours or until golden and cheese bubbles. Serves 8.

Patty Laughery
Moses Lake, WA

Cheesy Baked Spaghetti

Take Five!

You don't have to use every ingredient in your kitchen to whip up these wonderful recipes. They only use five to seven ingredients each! Most include some already-prepared items...like mixes, eggnog, frosting, or pizza crust...making these dishes extra quick to fix.

Easiest Pumpkin Cupcakes

Easiest Pumpkin Cupcakes

Short on time? Whip up these cupcakes in the blink of an eye using a spice cake mix.

18¼-oz. pkg. spice cake mix
15-oz. can pumpkin
3 eggs
⅓ c. oil
⅓ c. water
16-oz. container cream cheese frosting

Combine cake mix, pumpkin, eggs, oil and water in a large bowl. Blend with an electric mixer on medium speed for 2 minutes. Spoon batter into 24 paper-lined muffin cups, filling each ¾ full. Bake at 350 degrees for 18 to 22 minutes or until toothpick tests clean. Cool in pans for 10 minutes; remove to wire racks. Cool completely. Spread cupcakes with frosting. Makes 2 dozen.

Chocolate Eggnog

A great no-fuss recipe for jazzing up store-bought eggnog.

2 qts. eggnog
16-oz. can chocolate syrup
Optional: ½ c. light rum
1 c. whipping cream
2 T. powdered sugar
Garnish: baking cocoa

Combine eggnog, chocolate syrup and rum, if using, in a punch bowl, stirring well. Beat whipping cream with an electric mixer on high speed until foamy. Add powdered sugar; continue beating until stiff peaks form. Dollop whipped cream over eggnog; sift cocoa over top. Serve immediately. Makes 3 quarts.

Valarie Dennard
Palatka, FL

105

Use handy shortcuts such as ready-to-use pizza crust and canned soup to make Barbecue Chicken Pizza and Potato-Corn Chowder. S'more Bars are also simple to make, and always a hit!

Barbecue Chicken Pizza

Barbecue Chicken Pizza
When you need dinner fast, keep this quick favorite in mind.

12-inch Italian pizza crust
1 c. barbecue sauce
3 c. cooked chicken, shredded
1 c. shredded mozzarella cheese
1/2 c. shredded Cheddar cheese
Optional: chopped green onion

Place pizza crust on a lightly greased 12" pizza pan. Spread sauce over crust; arrange chicken on top. Sprinkle with cheeses. Bake at 450 degrees for 8 to 10 minutes, or until cheeses melt and crust is crisp. Garnish with green onions, if desired. Serves 4.

Ginny Bone
Saint Peters, MO

Apple-Baked Pork Chops
Add a baked sweet potato for a hearty, comforting meal!

4 (1/2-inch-thick) boneless pork
  chops
1/4 c. butter
2 red apples, cored and halved
3 T. brown sugar, packed
2 t. cinnamon

Arrange pork chops in a lightly greased 13"x9" baking pan; dot one tablespoon butter over each pork chop. Place one apple half cut-side down onto each pork chop; sprinkle with brown sugar and cinnamon. Bake at 350 degrees for 30 to 45 minutes or until pork chops are no longer pink inside. Serves 4.

Michelle McCauley
Garland, TX

Beef Brisket in a Bag
Pineapple juice and soy sauce are the secret ingredients that make this brisket taste wonderful.

3 to 4-lb. beef brisket
1/2 t. pepper
1/2 t. paprika
1 T. all-purpose flour
6-oz. can pineapple juice
3 T. soy sauce
1-oz. pkg. onion soup mix

Rub brisket with pepper and paprika. Place brisket, fat-side up, in a large oven bag; add flour to bag, turning to coat. Place bag in a 13"x9" baking pan. Combine pineapple juice, soy sauce and soup mix; pour mixture over brisket. Close bag with nylon tie provided; cut six, 1/2-inch slits in top. Bake at 325 degrees for 3 hours. Remove from oven; place brisket on cutting board and pour remaining bag contents into the baking pan. Slice brisket against the grain; arrange slices over juices in baking pan. Baste with juices; cover pan with aluminum foil and return to oven for an additional 1 1/2 hours or until fork tender, basting occasionally. Serves 8 to 10.

Meg Venema
Kirkland, WA

Potato-Corn Chowder

Short on time? Use a package of ready-cooked bacon instead.

2 10¾-oz. cans potato soup
2 14¾-oz. cans cream-style corn
8 slices bacon, crisply cooked and
    crumbled
Optional: 1 to 2 T. bacon drippings
½ to 1 c. milk
salt, pepper and garlic salt to
    taste
Garnish: fresh parsley, chopped

Combine soup and corn in a 3-quart slow cooker; add bacon and bacon drippings, if desired. Add milk until soup is of desired consistency; add salt, pepper and garlic salt to taste. Cover and cook on low setting for 2 to 3 hours or until hot. Sprinkle with parsley, if desired. Serves 6 to 8.

Jerry Bostian
Oelwein, IA

Potato-Corn Chowder

S'more Bars

S'more Bars

All the campfire flavor of s'mores…enjoy them anytime!

8 to 10 whole graham crackers
20-oz. pkg. brownie mix
2 c. mini marshmallows
1 c. semi-sweet chocolate chips
⅔ c. chopped pecans

Arrange graham crackers in a single layer in a greased 13"x9" baking pan, completely covering bottom of pan, overlapping slightly; set aside.
Prepare brownie mix according to package directions; spread carefully over graham crackers. Bake at 350 degrees for 30 to 35 minutes. Sprinkle marshmallows, chocolate chips and pecans over brownie layer; bake for an additional 5 minutes or until golden. Cool in pan on a wire rack; cut into bars. Makes 2 dozen.

Jo Ann

sensational citrus!

Remember the days when Santa would leave an orange in every Christmas stocking? With these flavorful recipes, citrus will be a Yuletide favorite again! Create rich Gingerbread with Lemon Sauce, Orange Meringue Pie or Velvety Lime Squares. For breakfast, everyone will enjoy Baked Texas Orange French Toast. Need a light dessert after a big holiday meal? Try Honey-Grapefruit Granita for a refreshing treat!

Gingerbread with Lemon Sauce

Nothing tastes like the holiday season more than homemade gingerbread!

1 c. molasses
1 c. hot water
½ c. brown sugar, packed
½ c. shortening
1 egg
2½ c. all-purpose flour
1 t. ground ginger
1 t. ground cloves
1 t. cinnamon
1½ t. baking soda
1½ t. baking powder
Garnish: whipped cream and
   lemon zest

Mix together molasses and hot water; set aside. Beat brown sugar and shortening in a large mixing bowl at medium speed with an electric mixer until fluffy. Add egg and beat until incorporated. Combine flour and remaining ingredients; add to brown sugar mixture alternately with molasses mixture, beginning and ending with flour mixture. Beat just until blended after each addition. Pour batter into a greased 9-inch square pan. Bake at 350 degrees for 35 to 45 minutes or until cake springs back when gently touched. Cut cake into squares and garnish, if desired; serve with Lemon Sauce. Makes 10 to 12 servings.

Lemon Sauce:
½ c. sugar
2 T. cornstarch
1 c. water
2 T. butter
1 T. lemon zest
1 T. lemon juice

Combine sugar and cornstarch in a medium saucepan; gradually stir in water. Bring to a boil over medium heat. Cook, stirring constantly, one minute or until thickened. Remove from heat; stir in remaining ingredients. Let cool until warm.

Kathie Williams
Oakland City, IN

Gingerbread with Lemon Sauce

Baked Texas Orange French Toast

Orange juice and zest give Baked Texas Orange French Toast a tangy sweetness, while Orange Meringue Pie will surprise your gang with its rich, mellow flavor.

Burst-of-Lemon Muffins
These sweet muffins are the perfect breakfast bread for your family get-together.

1³/₄ c. all-purpose flour
³/₄ c. sugar
1 t. baking powder
³/₄ t. baking soda
¹/₄ t. salt
8-oz. carton lemon yogurt
1 egg
¹/₃ c. butter, melted
1 T. lemon juice
2 T. lemon zest
¹/₂ c. flaked coconut
Optional: 2 T. poppy seed

In a large bowl, combine flour, sugar, baking powder, baking soda and salt. In a small bowl, combine yogurt, egg, butter, lemon juice, lemon zest, coconut and poppy seed, if desired. Add to dry ingredients; stir just until dry ingredients are moistened. Fill paper-lined muffin cups. Bake at 400 degrees for 18 to 22 minutes. Let muffins cool for 5 minutes; remove from pans. Pierce muffin tops; spoon Topping over each muffin before serving. Makes one dozen.

Topping:
¹/₃ c. lemon juice
¹/₄ c. sugar
¹/₄ c. flaked coconut, toasted

Combine lemon juice and sugar in a small saucepan. Cook over medium heat until sugar dissolves. Remove from heat; fold in coconut.

Polly Sonowski
Wooster, OH

Baked Texas Orange French Toast
Serve with crispy bacon for a big, country breakfast!

¹/₂ c. butter, melted
¹/₄ c. honey
2¹/₂ t. cinnamon, divided
6 eggs
¹/₄ c. sugar
1 c. half-and-half
1 c. orange juice
2 t. orange zest
16 slices Texas toast
6-oz. can frozen orange juice concentrate, thawed and heated
Garnish: powdered sugar and orange slices

In a small bowl, combine butter, honey and 2 teaspoons cinnamon. Pour mixture into each of 2 ungreased 15"x10" jelly-roll pans. Beat together eggs, sugar, half-and-half, orange juice, orange zest and remaining cinnamon. Dip bread slices into egg mixture and place in prepared pans in single layers. Pour any remaining egg mixture over bread. Bake at 400 degrees for 10 minutes, turn slices over and bake an additional 10 minutes or until golden. Serve with warm orange juice concentrate and garnish with powdered sugar and orange slices, if desired. Makes 8 to 10 servings.

Sherry Rogers
Stillwater, OK

110

Orange Meringue Pie

Here's a twist on the traditional Lemon Meringue Pie.

9-inch pie crust
1 c. orange juice
1 c. orange sections
1 T. orange zest
1 c. plus 6 T. sugar, divided
1/4 t. salt
5 T. cornstarch
3 egg yolks, beaten
2 T. lemon juice
2 T. butter
4 egg whites, room temperature
1/2 t. vanilla extract

Place pie crust into a 9" pie plate. Fold edges under and flute. Prick bottom and sides with a fork. Bake at 450 degrees until golden. Remove from oven and let cool on a wire rack. Reduce oven temperature to 325 degrees.

Whisk together orange juice, orange sections, orange zest, one cup sugar, salt and cornstarch in a medium saucepan. Cook over medium-low heat, whisking constantly until thickened. Place egg yolks in a small bowl; gradually add half of orange mixture to egg yolks, whisking constantly. Return egg yolk mixture to remaining orange mixture in pan; cook over medium heat 5 minutes or until thickened, stirring constantly. Remove from heat and stir in lemon juice and butter. Keep warm.

Beat egg whites and vanilla at high speed with an electric mixer until foamy. Beat in remaining sugar, one tablespoon at a time, until stiff peaks form. Set aside.

Pour orange filling into warm pie crust. Dollop meringue onto filling. Lightly spread dollops together in decorative swirls, completely sealing meringue to pie crust. Bake at 325 degrees for 22 to 25 minutes or until golden. Cool completely on a wire rack. Serves 8.

Patricia Wesson
Westminster, CO

Lemon-Lime Marmalade

This marmalade makes a great gift. Double or triple the recipe and spoon it into jelly jars and keep refrigerated for 2 to 3 weeks.

1 lemon, quartered and seeded
1 lime, quartered
1 1/2 c. sugar

Combine lemon and lime in a blender. Pulse until finely chopped; transfer to a medium microwave-safe bowl. Stir in sugar. Microwave, uncovered, on high 4 minutes; cool. Cover and refrigerate until ready to serve. Makes one cup.

mmmmm... the fragrance of orange peels!

Orange Meringue Pie

Velvety Lime Squares

This frosty treat can be made ahead and is guaranteed to be a hit.

3-oz. can flaked coconut, divided
2 c. vanilla wafer crumbs
1/4 c. butter, melted
2 T. sugar
2 3-oz. pkgs. lime gelatin mix
2 c. boiling water
6-oz. can frozen limeade
    concentrate
3 pts. vanilla ice cream, softened
1/8 t. salt
3 drops green food coloring
Optional: chopped pecans

Spread 1/2 cup coconut on a baking sheet; toast at 375 degrees until lightly golden, about 5 minutes; set aside.

Blend together remaining coconut, vanilla wafer crumbs, butter and sugar; press into an 11"x7" baking pan. Bake at 375 degrees for 6 to 7 minutes; cool.

Stir together gelatin and boiling water; mix until gelatin dissolves. Add limeade, ice cream, salt and food coloring, stirring until smooth. Pour over crust; sprinkle with reserved toasted coconut and pecans, if desired. Cover and freeze until firm. Let stand at room temperature a few minutes before serving. Makes 15 servings.

Kathy Unruh
Fresno, CA

Orange-Ginger Biscotti

These crispy cookies are perfect for dipping in tea. Wrap a handful in cellophane bags and give as gifts.

2/3 c. almonds
2 c. all-purpose flour
2 t. ground ginger
2 t. baking powder
1/4 c. butter, softened
1/2 c. brown sugar, packed
6 T. plus 2 t. sugar
2 T. orange zest
2 eggs, divided and beaten
1/2 t. vanilla extract
2/3 c. pistachios, chopped

Finely grind almonds, flour, ginger and baking powder in a food processor; set aside.

Beat butter in a large bowl at medium speed with an electric mixer until creamy; gradually add brown sugar and 6 tablespoons sugar, beating until light and fluffy. Add zest, one egg yolk and vanilla; beat until smooth. Gradually add almond mixture, beating until blended. Stir in pistachios.

Divide dough in half. Using floured hands, roll each half on a lightly floured surface into a 1/2-inch thick log. Arrange logs 4 inches apart on a greased and floured baking sheet. Cover with plastic wrap; refrigerate for one hour.

Brush dough with remaining egg yolk; sprinkle with remaining sugar. Bake at 350 degrees for 30 minutes or until golden and firm to the touch. Let cool for 10 minutes. Using a serrated knife, cut logs crosswise into 1/2-inch thick slices. Arrange slices cut-sides down on baking sheet. Bake at 300 degrees until golden on top, about 12 minutes. Turn over; bake an additional 12 minutes or until golden brown. Transfer biscotti to a wire rack; cool completely. Store in an airtight container at room temperature. Makes 1 1/2 dozen.

Carrie O'Shea
Marina Del Ray, CA

Velvety Lime Squares

Smooth and creamy Velvety Lime Squares will disappear in a hurry! And of course, we couldn't celebrate the goodness of citrus without including grapefruit! Honey-Grapefruit Granita is simple to make, pretty to serve, and just plain delicious.

Honey-Grapefruit Granita

Here's a new way to highlight one of the season's best citrus fruits. It's so refreshing!

2 c. sugar
2 c. water
4 c. fresh pink grapefruit juice
1/3 c. honey, warmed

Combine sugar and water in a large saucepan; bring to a boil. Cook until sugar dissolves, stirring constantly; cool. Combine sugar mixture, grapefruit juice and honey; stir well. Pour into a 13"x9" baking dish. Cover with plastic wrap; place in freezer. Freeze 8 hours, scraping occasionally, until frozen. Makes 6 cups.

Tiffany Brinkley
Broomfield, CO

Honey-Grapefruit Granita

Key Lime-White Chocolate Chippers

These tasty cookies taste just like Key lime pie. Leave a plateful for Santa as a special treat.

1/2 c. butter, softened
1 c. sugar
1 egg
1 egg yolk
2 c. all-purpose flour
1 t. baking powder
1/2 t. salt
1/4 c. lime juice
1 1/2 t. lime zest
3/4 c. white chocolate chips

In a large bowl, beat butter, sugar, egg and egg yolk at medium speed with an electric mixer. Add flour, baking powder, salt, lime juice and lime zest. Stir in chocolate chips. Roll dough into walnut-size balls. Place 2 inches apart on lightly greased baking sheets. Bake at 350 degrees for 8 to 10 minutes. Makes 2 1/2 dozen.

Cora Baker
La Rue, OH

Project Instructions

Sleigh with Trees
(also shown on page 9)

Place balled and burlapped saplings in the family sleigh. Decorate the trees with colorful Cardinal and Bell Mini-Banner ornaments.

Sweater Throw
(also shown on page 10)
- assorted red and green knit sweaters (we used 9 different sweaters)

- red flannel for backing and binding (we used 3¼ yards of 43"w flannel for our 45"x60" throw)
- red embroidery floss

Match right sides and use a ½" seam allowance when sewing unless otherwise indicated.

1. Cut the sleeves from the sweaters and cut open the sleeve seams. Trim all the knit pieces to the same width. Stabilize the knit pieces by zigzagging around the edges, using a medium stitch length and width.

2. Arrange the knit pieces in horizontal rows. Zigzag the pieces together (along the short ends) one row at a time. Trim the rows to the same length; then, zigzag the rows together to complete the top.

3. Cut a flannel piece the same size as the top, piecing as necessary. Matching the *wrong* sides, baste the top to the flannel backing along the outer edges. Use floss lengths to tie the top and backing together.

4. For the binding, cut a 3½"w flannel strip the same length as 1 long edge of the throw. Press ½" to the wrong side along 1 long edge. Matching right sides, sew the long raw edge of the binding to the throw edge. Fold the pressed edge to the throw wrong side and slipstitch the binding to the backing. Repeat for the remaining long edge.

5. Cut a 3½"w flannel strip the length of 1 short end of the throw, plus 1". Press ½" to the wrong side along 1 long edge and both ends. Matching right sides, sew the long raw edge of the binding to the throw edge. Fold the pressed edge to the throw wrong side and slipstitch the binding to the backing. Repeat for the remaining short end.

Lamp Post Banner
(also shown on page 11)
- 17½"x45" piece of primed canvas
- transfer paper
- apple green, green, brown, dark brown, red and ivory acrylic paints and paint brushes
- satin interior/exterior varnish
- six 25mm red jingle bells

1. Fold the canvas side and bottom edges 1" to the wrong side; machine stitch. For the casing, fold the top edge 3" to the wrong side and machine stitch close to the raw edge.

2. Enlarge the pattern (page 148) to 455%. Use transfer paper to transfer the design to both sides of the hemmed canvas. Paint the design on both sides. Apply several coats of varnish to the banner.

3. Sew the jingle bells along the banner bottom edge.

Bell Mini-Banner Ornament

(also shown on page 12)
- red vinyl
- apple green felt
- pinking shears
- ivory acrylic paint and round paintbrush
- three 25mm green jingle bells
- 1½" D-ring
- fabric glue
- 15mm silver jingle bell
- twill tape

1. Use pinking shears to cut a 2¼"x6¼" felt piece and the long edges of a 2"x12" vinyl piece.
2. Matching the short ends, fold the vinyl in half. Slide the felt piece between the vinyl layers and trim the upper corners of the felt and vinyl. Paint dots on the vinyl. Sew the green jingle bells to the top vinyl layer.
3. Slip the D-ring between the vinyl and felt layers. Glue the layers together. Knot the silver bell to the D-ring with twill tape.

Sleigh Bell Strap

(also shown on page 13)
- 4" dia. brass ring
- silver spray paint
- 5"x32" piece of red vinyl
- fabric glue
- 16" length of 3"w apple green ribbon
- four 2½" silver jingle bells
- 45 assorted size silver jingle bells
- 30-gauge silver wire
- artificial greenery
- 1½ yards 1½"w red dotted reversible ribbon

1. Working in a well-ventilated area, spray the brass ring silver.
2. Enlarge pattern (page 147) to 158%. Use the pattern and cut the strap from the vinyl. Cut the ribbon slits on the front side only of the strap.
3. Thread the green ribbon through the slits; glue on the wrong side. Sew the large jingle bells to the ribbon. Thread the strap through the silver ring, match the scalloped edges and glue the vinyl together.
4. Thread assorted silver jingle bells onto lengths of wire, wrapping the wire after each bell and allowing a bit of space before adding the next one. Wire the greenery pieces and the bell wires to the ring top. Make a multi-loop bow and attach to the ring top with a ribbon length.

Printed Tree Skirt

(continued from page 17)
3. Follow *Making and Using Wood Letter Stamps* (pages 137-138) to make stamps for "Glad Tidings." Use stamps and permanent ink to stamp letters across the center front about 6" from the outer edge.
4. Finger press the upholstery webbing raw ends ½" to the wrong side twice; then, hand sew the hems with the embroidery floss. To pleat the webbing, follow Fig. 1 to pin inverted pleats along entire length. Use floss to hand sew the pleated webbing around the skirt's outer edge. Sew rickrack and buttons to the skirt.

Fig. 1

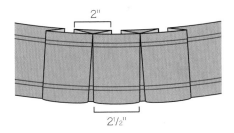

Jar Lid Ornament

(also shown on page 17)
- zinc jar lid
- hammer, nail, and scrap of wood
- curly ornament hanger
- acetate
- India ink and quill (available with the art supplies)
- toothpick
- craft glue
- white cardstock
- mica flakes
- tinsel sticks
- mini vintage ornaments
- red twill tape
- printed paper tinsel

1. To attach the wire hanger to the jar lid, place the lid on the wood scrap and use the nail to punch 2 holes (Fig. 1). Insert the wire ornament hanger through the holes in the lid.

Fig. 1

2. Cut a circle of acetate to fit in the jar lid opening. Trace the desired pattern (page 147) onto the acetate with the India ink and quill. Set aside to dry. Lines can be "cleaned up" by gently scraping the dry ink away with a toothpick.

3. Glue a cardstock circle to the inside of the jar lid. Sprinkle mica flakes in the lid. With the inked side down, glue the acetate circle into the jar lid rim. Run a thin bead of glue outside the acetate circle and sprinkle more mica flakes into the wet glue.

4. Decorate the hanger with tinsel sticks, mini vintage ornaments, red twill tape and paper tinsel.

Framed Pen & Ink Scene

(continued from page 21)

2. Cut a piece of linen the same size as the frame backing. Using 6 strands of floss, center and stitch a 7"x5" *Backstitch* (page 138) "frame" on the linen. Stamp HOME under the stitched frame. For the snowflakes, dot the linen with craft glue (staying within the stitched area) and adhere mica flakes.

3. Working in a well-ventilated area, use spray adhesive to adhere the stamped and stitched linen to the frame backing. Reassemble the frame with the inked glass (inked side against the linen) and the linen-covered backing.

Good Cheer Garland

(also shown on page 21)
- craft foam
- wood scraps
- craft glue
- solvent-based permanent ink pad, such as StazOn®
- fabric for backgrounds (we used a heavy linen)
- embroidery floss
- lightweight fusible interfacing
- twelve 1/4" grommets
- 5 yards of 1 1/2"w ribbon
- 2 yards of 3/8"w ribbon for ties

1. Follow *Making and Using Wood Letter Stamps* (pages 137-138) to make stamps for an asterisk and "Good Cheer." (For size reference, our asterisk is 3" high, our G is 8" high, our C is 6" high and our d and h are 2 1/4" high.) Use stamps and permanent ink to stamp each letter on the background fabric. Leave 3 1/4" above each stamped image and 1" on each side and the bottom of the image for trimming and finishing.

2. Trim the stamped images apart, leaving a margin of 3 1/4" above each image and about 1" on each side and the bottom. Press the top fabric edges 1 1/2" to the right side. Using 6 strands of floss, work *Running Stitches* (page 139) near the bottom edges. Fuse interfacing to the wrong sides of the fabric pieces. Attach grommets to the tops of the fabric pieces.

3. Thread the large letters onto the wide ribbon and use the narrow ribbon to tie the small letters and the asterisk to the wide ribbon.

Felted Wool Acorn
(continued from page 25)

1. To cover the foam ball or egg with roving, pour 6 cups hot water in a plastic basin; mix in 1 tablespoon liquid dishwashing detergent. Tear roving into 3" to 4" long sections and pull sections apart into 3-4 pieces.

2. Dip a foam ball or egg in the water. Use wet fingers to tightly wrap a few roving pieces around the wet ball or egg (Fig. 1).

Fig. 1

3. Keeping fingers and ball wet, but not saturated, add more roving, wrapping in different directions (Fig. 2).

Fig. 2

4. For the ball to have an acorn shape, add more roving at the ball bottom (Fig. 3). Repeat until the ball or egg is well covered (some shrinkage will occur as it dries). Allow the ball or egg to dry overnight.

Fig. 3

5. To give the acorn cap dimension, wrap the cord around the top half of the ball or egg, starting in the center and gluing as you wrap (Fig. 4).

Fig. 4

6. Wrap the rickrack around the ball or egg (Fig. 5), completely covering the cord, starting just under the cord and gluing as you wrap.

Fig. 5

7. When you reach the top, create a stem by folding the rickrack down into the center. Pin in place. Fold

and glue the rickrack end over the pin (Fig. 6).

Fig. 6

Mistletoe Tea Towel
(also shown on page 25)
- tissue paper
- tea towel
- white, green and light green embroidery floss
- white felt
- 1/4" dia. hole punch
- ribbon for bow
- ribbons and rickrack to trim towel
- clear nylon thread

1. Transfer (page 137) the pattern (page 145) to the towel.
2. Use 3 strands of floss to work *Chain Stitch* (page 139) stems and leaves and *Stem Stitch* leaf veins. Punch berries from felt. Using 6 strands of floss, work *French Knots* to attach berries. Sew a knotted ribbon bow to the stems.
3. Use clear thread to sew the ribbons and rickrack to the towel's bottom edge.

Window Dressing Garlands
(also shown on page 29)
Bring a bit of snowflake magic indoors with this frosty window or mirror dressing.

Enlarge the patterns (page 143) to 200%. Use the enlarged patterns and cut snowflakes from felt. Sew vintage buttons to the snowflake centers. Thread the snowflakes, more vintage buttons and pom-poms onto 30-lb. test weight fishing line lengths, knotting the line above and below each element.

Fun & Games Tree
(also shown on page 31)

Add a cheery touch to the children's playroom with a child-size tree decorated with ornaments made from vintage toys and displayed in a brightly colored wagon. Red corduroy fabric tucked around the tree base serves as a tree skirt. Fill the wagon with packages to create a movable holiday decoration for children of all ages.

Turtle Tic-Tac-Toe Toss
(also shown on page 33)
Supplies and instructions are for six turtles and one game mat

- 12"x18" sheet **each** of green and light green felt
- green and light green embroidery floss
- polyester fiberfill
- yellow, blue, light green and coral medium weight yarn
- dried beans
- 24"x24" square of red felt
- 3 yards of 1"w blue ribbon
- fabric marking pen

1. To make the Turtles, enlarge the patterns (pages 141) to 200%. Using the enlarged patterns, cut 6 heads, 6 shells, 3 tails and 24 legs **each** from green and light green felt.

2. Matching the raw edges and working ⅛" from edges, use green floss and *Running Stitches* (page 139) to sew 2 green legs together leaving the straight edge open; stuff with fiberfill. Make 12 green legs. Repeat with light green floss and legs.

3. Repeat Step 2 to make 3 green and 3 light green heads. For eyes, thread a needle with light green or blue yarn; knot one yarn end and sew straight through the head. Knot the yarn close to the opposite side of the head; cut the yarn.

4. Leaving the beginning knot on the right side, use blue yarn to work 2 *Running Stitch* circles and a *Satin Stitch* dot in the centers of 3 light green shells. Use yellow yarn to work 8 *Lazy Daisies* around each larger circle.

5. In the center of 3 green shells, work a large "X" using 2 strands of light green yarn; tack the "X" center to the shell with a *Straight Stitch*. Work 4 *Lazy Daisies* with light green yarn. Leaving the beginning knots on the right side, work 4 coral *Lazy Daisies* on the shell.

6. Fold tail as shown in Fig. 1; pin.

Fig. 1

7. Matching the *wrong* sides and raw edges, layer 1 light green plain shell and 1 light green embroidered shell. Pin 4 green legs, 1 green head and 1 green tail between the shells. Using green floss and leaving an opening for inserting beans, whipstitch the shells together, catching the head, legs, and tail in the stitching. Fill the shell with beans and sew the opening closed. Make 3 turtles with light green shells and 3 turtles with green shells.

8. To make the game mat, cut ribbon into four 24" lengths. Leaving the beginning knots on the right side, work yellow yarn *Running Stitches* to attach the ribbons 2½" from the red felt square edges; trim each ribbon end at an angle. Draw a nine-block grid of 6½" squares (Fig. 2). Work yellow yarn *Running Stitches* over the drawn lines.

Fig. 2

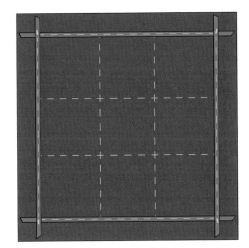

Horsie
(continued from page 32)
Match right sides, raw edges and use a ½" seam allowance for all sewing.

1. Center and fuse the interfacing to the wrong sides of the T-shirt and sweater pieces.

2. Enlarge the patterns (pages 142 and 143) to 250%. Using the enlarged gusset pattern, cut 1 gusset from the T-shirt piece. Using the enlarged body pattern, cut 2 bodies from the sweater pieces. Transfer the pattern markings to the wrong sides of the pieces.

3. Fuse web to the remaining T-shirt scraps. Using the enlarged pattern, cut 2 ears from the striped knit. Fuse the ears to the green felt and cut out about ½" beyond the striped ears.

4. For the back seam, sew the bodies together from the nose dot to the tail dot. To shape the nose, fold and stitch across a small triangle of fabric where the face curves (Fig. 1).

Fig. 1

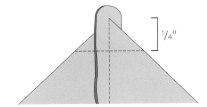

5. Matching the dots, pin the gusset and body pieces together. Leaving an opening for turning between one set of stars, sew the gusset to the body. Clip the curves and turn right side out.

6. Place a bag of beans in each foot and in the tummy area; stuff tightly with fiberfill. Hand sew the opening closed.

7. For the eyes, cut 2 ⅝" circles from the blue felt. Pin the eyes in place. Using yellow yarn and leaving the beginning knot on the surface, run the needle through the center of one eye, through the head and come out in the opposite eye center. Knot the yarn close to the surface and trim. Work a *Stem Stitch* (page 139) mouth and *Straight Stitch* eyelashes with brown floss.

8. For the tail, cut 28 18" yarn lengths; tie together at the center with another yarn piece. Place the bundle over the body/gusset intersection; tack in place and trim yarn ends.

9. For the mane, cut 180 9" yarn lengths. Separate yarn into 20 bundles of 9 lengths each. Beginning at the square on the forehead, place a bundle center over the seam. Use green floss to work a few *Backstitches* over the bundle (Fig. 4). Place a second bundle next to the first; work *Backstitches* over the second bundle. Continue attaching the remaining bundles. Trim the yarn ends.

Fig. 4

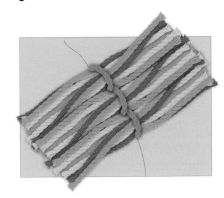

10. Pleat the bottom straight edge of each ear. Use green embroidery floss to sew the ears to the head.

Piggie
(also shown on page 32)

- two 13"x16" pieces of striped knit fabric cut from a gently used sweater
- 14"x16" rectangle of cotton print fabric
- two 12"x15" rectangles of lightweight fusible interfacing
- fabric marking pen
- paper-backed fusible web
- pink and light green felt
- 5 small plastic zipping bags loosely filled with dried beans
- 9" of ¼" wide pink ribbon
- brown embroidery floss
- blue yarn
- polyester fiberfill

Match right sides, raw edges and use a ¹/₂" seam allowance for all sewing.

1. Center and fuse the interfacing to the wrong sides of the sweater pieces.
2. Enlarge the patterns (pages 143 and 144) to 146%. Using the enlarged gusset pattern, cut a gusset from the cotton piece. Using the enlarged body pattern, cut 2 bodies from the sweater pieces. Transfer the pattern markings to the wrong sides of the pieces.
3. Fuse the web to the remaining cotton scraps. Using the enlarged patterns, cut 2 ears from cotton. Fuse the ears to the pink felt and cut out about ¼" beyond the cotton ears.

4. For the back seam, sew the bodies together from the snout dot to the tail dot.
5. Matching the dots, pin the gusset and body pieces together. Leaving an opening for turning between one set of stars, sew the gusset to the body. Clip the curves and turn right side out.
6. Press under ¹/₂" on the nose. Pin the nose over the snout opening and slipstitch in place.
7. Place a bag of beans in each foot and in the tummy area; stuff tightly with fiberfill. Hand sew the opening closed.
8. For the eyes, cut 2 ¹/₂" circles from the green felt. Pin the eyes in place. Using blue yarn and leaving the beginning knot on the surface, run the needle through the center of one eye, through the head and come out in the opposite eye. Knot the yarn close to surface and trim. Work a *Stem Stitch* (page 139) mouth and *Straight Stitch* nostrils and eyelashes with brown floss.
9. For the tail, tie a knot at each end of the pink ribbon; tack the tail at the body/gusset intersection.
10. Pleat the bottom straight edge of each ear. Use pink embroidery floss to sew ears to the head.

Gift Cubes
(continued from page 33)

3. Matching the short ends and beginning and ending at the dots, refer to Fig. 1 to sew the red rectangles and squares together.

Fig. 1

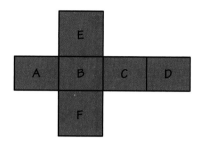

4. To form the cube, sew A and E, then A and F together. Sew E and C, then F and C together to make a box with one open side. Press the raw edges of D ¹/₂" to the wrong side. Insert a foam cube into the box. Fold D over the opening and slipstitch in place.
5. Overlapping and gluing the ends at the top center, wrap the cube with a 40" ribbon length. Loop an 18" ribbon length into a bow and stack on a 24" long streamer. Wrap a 6" ribbon length around the bow center and glue the ends together. Glue the bow and a pom-pom to the cube.
6. Repeat Steps 2-5 with blue corduroy, remaining foam cube, ribbon and pom-pom.

Star Ornament/Tree Topper
(also shown on page 34)

- tracing paper
- assorted colors felt
- wood spools and sticks (we used vintage Tinkertoys®)
- wood glue
- assorted size and colors wood beads

1. Using the patterns on page 142, cut a small star from felt. For the larger ornament or tree topper, also cut a large star from felt.

2. Insert sticks into the spool holes to form star shapes. Glue additional sticks to the spool edges. Glue a bead to the end of each stick.

3. Glue the small felt star to the back of the ornament. Glue a large felt star over the small star for the large ornament. Glue a large bead to the ornament front.

Bead Garland
(also shown on page 34)

Your little ones will have fun while learning shapes and colors when they help craft this easy garland. Using the patttern on page 142, cut stars from felt. Use decorative-edged scissors to cut 1³/₄" diameter felt circles. Punch an ¹/₈" diameter hole in the center of each felt shape. Knot 1 end of a multi-colored hemp twine length and thread on a small wood bead, a jumbo wood bead and then a felt shape. Continue alternating jumbo beads and felt shapes until garland is the desired length, ending with a small bead and a knot.

Personalized Tree Ornaments
(also shown on page 34)
• wood logs and slats (we used vintage Lincoln Logs™)
• wood spools (we used vintage Tinkertoys®)
• wood glue
• fine-tooth handsaw
• sandpaper
• green acrylic paint and paintbrush
• wood letter tiles (we used pieces from a vintage Scrabble® game)
• assorted sizes and colors wood beads
• 6-ply multi-colored hemp twine

1. For the tree trunk, glue a wood log to the flat side of a spool (we used 4¹/₂" long logs, but you can adjust the length of the logs to fit the desired name).

2. For the branches, cut slats into 2", 3" and 4" long pieces (for taller trees cut more braches, increasing the length in 1" increments). Sand and drybrush (page 138) the ends with green paint. Spacing the branches one letter tile height apart, glue the branches to the trunk. Glue the letter tiles on and between the branches.

3. Glue beads to the branches and tree top.

4. For the hangers, knot the ends of a twine length together. Glue the ends in the top bead hole.

Button Wreath
(also shown on page 38)
• sturdy 14" wire ring, cut open with wire cutters
• 1¹/₂ yards total of assorted green 36" wide felt
• ³/₄ yard total of assorted green 44/45" wide fabrics
• craft knife
• heavy-duty masking tape
• assorted green vintage buttons
• 2 felt flower ornaments (page 39)
• gathered rickrack ornament (page 39)
• tree topper size flower ornament (page 39)

1. Cut 104 4" felt squares. Cut 104 3" fabric squares. Fold and slit a felt square as shown in Fig. 1. Thread the folded square onto the wire ring. Repeat with the remaining squares, alternating fabric and felt.

Fig. 1

2. Securely tape the ring ends together and adjust the squares to cover the tape. Sew buttons to some of the squares and clip the ornaments to the wreath.

Flower Ornament/Tree Topper

(also shown on page 39)
- ¼ yard fabric for flower petals
- fabric scraps for leaf and flower center
- felt scrap
- button
- craft glue
- clothespin

1. For petals, cut six 5"x5" pieces of petal fabric. Matching the wrong sides, fold a fabric square in half diagonally, fold the side points to the center and finally, fold the corner Point A's to the back (Figs. 1-3). Use *Running Stitches* (page 139) to baste along the raw edge (Fig. 3). Tightly gather the basting thread and securely knot. Repeat with the remaining fabric squares.

Fig. 1

Fig. 2

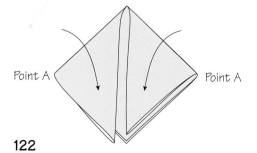

Point A   Point A

Fig. 3

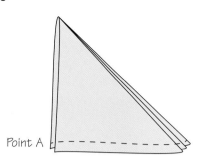

Point A

2. Cut a 2" diameter felt circle and 1½" diameter fabric circle. Glue the petals to the felt circle. Sew the fabric circle and button to the flower center.

3. For the leaf, fold and slit a 5"x5" fabric square as shown in Fig. 4. Whipstitch through the slit, cinching the leaf. Glue the leaf to the flower back. Glue the clothespin to the leaf.

Fig. 4

4. For the tree topper, follow Steps 1-3 using 7"x7" fabric squares for the petals, a 2½" diameter felt circle, a 1¾" diameter fabric circle and a 6"x6" fabric square for the leaf.

Gathered Rickrack Ornament

(also shown on page 39)
- 58" length of jumbo rickrack
- matching embroidery floss
- button
- felt scrap
- small clothespin
- craft glue

1. Use floss to work *Running Stitches* (page 139) along 1 long edge of the rickrack (Fig. 1). Pull the thread to tightly gather the rickrack, forming a flower; tack the rickrack together on the back and securely knot the thread. Glue as necessary on the flower wrong side to maintain the shape. Sew the button to the flower center.

Fig. 1

2. Enlarge the leaf pattern (page 141) to 200%. Use the enlarged pattern to cut a felt leaf. Glue the leaf and the clothespin to the flower back.

Blooming Apron

(also shown on page 41)

- 1¼ yards of fabric for ties, waistband and ruffle
- 14"x12" fabric piece for bib
- 28"x16" fabric piece for skirt
- fabric scrap for bib trim
- pinking shears
- ½ yard fabric for lining
- 3½ yards rickrack
- vintage hankie
- 3¾ yards 1"w ribbon
- green felt scrap
- light green acrylic paint
- liner paintbrush
- twill tape
- gathered fabric ornament (page 39) without clothespin

Match right sides and use a ½" seam allowance for all sewing unless otherwise indicated.

1. Cut two 4"x87" waistband/tie strips (these will have to be pieced) and a 6½"x70" ruffle strip (this will have to be pieced) and two 22"x4" straps. Set the waistband/tie and ruffle strips aside.

2. Matching the long edges, fold each strap in half and sew the long edge and 1 short end together. Turn right side out and press. Matching the raw edges, pin the straps to 1 long edge of the bib, placing the straps 1" from the side edges.

3. Use pinking shears to trim the fabric scrap to a 5"x5" square. Turn diagonally and center the square on the bib top edge; baste in place and trim excess fabric. Cut a 14"x12" lining piece for the bib. Leaving the bottom edge open, sew the bib pieces together. Turn right side out and press.

4. Sew rickrack to 2 hankie edges. Fold the hankie in half diagonally. Pin the hankie to the bib with the fold 1" below the top edge. Raise the top layer of the hankie and topstitch the hankie along the top edge of the bib.

5. For the skirt ruffle, match the long edges and fold the ruffle fabric piece in half. Sew the side seams. Turn right side out and press. Baste along the raw edge at ½" and ¼"; pull the basting threads, gathering the ruffle to 27". Center and sew the ruffle to the skirt bottom edge.

6. Cut a 28"x16" lining piece for the skirt. Leaving the top edge open, sew the skirt pieces together. Turn right side out and press.

7. Matching the raw edges, center, pin, and then sew the bib to a waistband/tie strip. Repeat to sew the skirt to the bottom of the strip. Matching right sides, pin the remaining waistband/tie strip to the first strip. Leaving the skirt and bib areas unstitched, sew along the long edges and short ends of the ties. Clip the corners, turn right side out and press, turning the raw edges of the waistband under ½". Pin, then topstitch the waistband area.

8. Pin, then sew ribbon and rickrack to the center of the waistband/ties, turning the ends ½" to the wrong side.

9. Turning the ends ½" to the wrong side and whipstitching in place, twist and tack the remaining ribbon over the ruffle seam.

10. Enlarge the holly leaf pattern from the Mini Pennant Swag (page 141) to 200%. Use the enlarged pattern to cut 2 felt holly leaves. Paint the leaf veins. Sew the leaves, a twill tape bow and the gathered fabric ornament to the bib.

Mini Pennant Swag

(also shown on page 40)

- assorted fabric scraps at least 7"x7" (we used vintage feed sacks)
- paper-backed fusible web
- red felt (8"x8" for each triangle)
- green felt (4"x4" for each holly leaf set)
- light green acrylic paint
- liner paintbrush
- jumbo rickrack
- fabric glue
- red vintage buttons

1. Fuse the web to the wrong side of the fabric scraps.

2. Enlarge the patterns (page 141) to 200%. Using the enlarged triangle pattern, cut the fabric triangles. Fuse the fabric triangles to the felt. Cut out each felt triangle about ⅛" from the fabric.

3. Use the enlarged holly leaf pattern to cut sets of 2 holly leaves. Paint the leaf veins.

4. Glue the triangles to a rickrack length. Sew the buttons and holly leaves to the banner.

Farmgirl Doll

(also shown on page 41)
- 1/4 yard muslin
- 1/8 yard fabric for body
- 1/3 yard vintage fabric for apron
- vintage fabric scrap for overskirt
- felt scrap for shoes
- rickrack, buttons and ribbon
- transfer paper
- embroidery floss
- pink crayon
- 78 yards sportweight yarn
- fabric glue
- polyester fiberfill
- soft sculpture needle
- heavy-duty thread

Always match right sides and use a 1/4" seam allowance when sewing, unless otherwise indicated.

1. Enlarge the patterns (page 141) to 200%. Using the patterns, cut the head, arms, and legs from muslin and the shoes from felt. Cut the body pieces.

2. Transfer the face to 1 head piece. Work *Stem Stitches* (page 139) and *Straight Stitches* for the facial features. Color in the cheeks with crayon.

3. Sew 1 head piece to each body piece. Sew the head and body pieces together, leaving the bottom edge open.

4. Press the body bottom edges 1/4" to the wrong side. Stuff the head and body with fiberfill.

5. For the hair, cut 141 18" yarn lengths. Lay the yarn lengths side by side on a 5" high scrap piece of paper; some of the yarn pieces will overlap. Sew down the center of the yarn, sewing through both the yarn and the paper (Fig. 1); tear the paper away. Glue the hair to the head.

Fig. 1

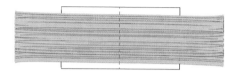

6. Divide each side of hair into 3 sections and braid, tying a small piece of yarn at the braid end. Tie a ribbon over the yarn tie. Trim the ribbon and hair ends.

7. Sew 2 leg pieces together, leaving the top open; clip the curves, turn right side out and firmly stuff with fiberfill to 1" from the top edge. Sew across the leg right above the fiberfill. Repeat with the remaining leg pieces. Insert the legs into the body 1/4"; topstitch across the body bottom, catching the legs in the stitching.

8. Sew 2 arm pieces together, leaving an opening for turning. Clip the curves, turn right side out and firmly stuff with fiberfill. Sew the opening closed. Repeat with the remaining arm pieces. Using the soft sculpture needle and heavy-duty thread, sew the arms to the body (Fig. 2).

Fig. 2

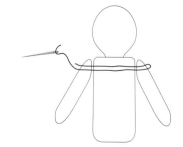

9. For the apron, use the enlarged pattern and cut 2 bibs. Cut a 15"x5 1/4" skirt, a 2 1/2"x24" waistband/tie and a 4 1/2"x4 3/4" overskirt. Sew the bib pieces together, leaving the strap ends and the bib bottom open. Clip the corners, turn right side out and press. Sew the buttons to the bib.

10. Matching the long edges, fold the waistband/ties piece in half and sew together, leaving an opening for turning. Clip the corners, turn right side out and press. Sew the opening closed. Center a rickrack length on the waistband; use clear thread to zigzag in place.

11. Press 1/4" to the wrong side twice on the side and bottom edges of the skirt and overskirt; topstitch. Use clear thread to zigzag rickrack to the overskirt. Center and baste the overskirt to the skirt along the top edge. Gather the skirt to 7".

12 . Center the skirt and bib on the waistband/tie wrong side (Fig. 3). Pin the bib straps in place. Topstitch along the top and bottom edges of the waistband.

Fig. 3

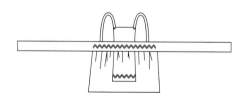

13. For the shoes, use the enlarged pattern and cut 2 shoe fronts and 2 shoe backs (don't cut opening in shoe backs). Sew a shoe front to each shoe back, leaving the top open. Clip the curves and turn right side out. Slip the shoes on the doll's feet.

Use floss to sew a cluster of 5-7 beads to each group of 2 leaves. Glue a clothespin to the wrong side.

6. Arrange the greenery, tree and birdcages. Clip the star, some ornaments and birds to the tree and on the birdcages. Clip the holly clusters and ornaments to the twill tape and arrange among the greenery.

All Aflutter

(also shown on page 43)

- assorted double-sided cardstock
- glitter
- craft glue
- colored plastic mini-clothespins
- red and green beads
- embroidery floss
- disposable foam brush
- glitter-branch decorative tree
- vintage birdcages
- assorted greenery
- red twill tape

1. Enlarge the patterns (page 149) to 200%. Use the enlarged patterns to cut the pieces from cardstock.

2. For each bird, dot the eyes with glue and sprinkle with glitter. Highlight the cardstock design with a bit of glitter. Glue a clothespin to the wrong side of one body piece. Glue the body pieces together along the head and upper edges; add the wings and folded tail.

3. For each ball ornament, use floss to sew a cluster of 5 beads on a cardstock circle. Glue a clothespin to the wrong side of the ornament.

4. Brush glue on the star and sprinkle with glitter. Glue a clothespin to the wrong side.

5. Enlarge the holly leaf pattern from the Mini Pennant Swag (page 141) to 350%. Use the enlarged pattern to cut 2 leaves for each holly grouping. Fold each leaf and sharply crease the fold.

Tree Stocking

(also shown on page 47)

- two 14"x23" pieces of green felt
- pinking shears
- vintage tablecloth with large motif
- fabric glue
- assorted rickrack
- assorted buttons
- clear nylon thread

1. Enlarge the Poinsettias Stocking pattern (page 150, ignoring the poinsettia design) to 206%. Use the enlarged pattern and pinking shears to cut 2 green felt stocking pieces. For the hanger, cut a 1"x5" felt piece; set aside.

2. Trim ½" from all edges of the pattern. Using the trimmed pattern, decide placement of the motif and cut the tablecloth stocking piece. Glue the rickrack to the toe and cuff areas. Sew buttons on the cuff and tree.

3. Centering the tablecloth piece on top, stack the stocking pieces and use clear thread to zigzag all 3 layers together, leaving the top edge open. Glue the top edge of the tablecloth stocking in place. Sew a button and the hanger to the upper right corner.

Counting the Days Calendar

(also shown on page 48)

Paint a 12"x12" square wood plaque; glue a ribbon border around the edges. Adhere letter stickers, spelling "Merry Christmas," on 1¼" punched cardstock circles. Paint and then decorate a 4"x4" wood square with scrapbook paper, burlap and stickers. Glue the letters and wood square to the plaque. Attach layered cardstock backgrounds using long nails to the left of the square. Hang number tags (use stickers for the numbers and trims) on the nails to count down the days to Christmas.

Matchbox Garland
(also shown on page 48)

Use decorative papers, ribbons, 3-D embellishments and number stickers to decorate small matchboxes. Place a Christmas treat in each box and glue a twill tape hanger to the inside back of the box cover. Attach each hanger to a ribbon garland with a small brad. We also mixed in a few vintage children's nursery rhyme rubber stamps. Bells, charms and tiny ornaments tied on with floss top off each hanger.

Mini Gift Sacks
(also shown on page 49)

Matching short ends and right sides, fold a 4"x9¹/₂" fabric piece in half. Use a ¹/₄" seam allowance to sew the side seams, catching a piece of twill tape in one side seam. Turn the sack right side out and press the top edge ³/₄" to the inside. Leaving a long tail at the beginning and end, start at one seam and work embroidery floss *Running Stitches* (page 139) around the top edge; trim and knot the ends together to complete the drawstring. Use an office-type date stamp, small charms, mini safety pins, embroidery stitches, ornaments and buttons to decorate the twill tape labels.

Handmade Boxes
Open Window Cookie Box
(also shown on page 53)
- transfer paper
- patterned cardstock
- stylus or bone folder
- double-sided tape
- wrapped cookies
- ribbon
- rub-on message
- embroidery floss

1. Enlarge the pattern on page 154 to 200%. *Transfer (page 137) the pattern to cardstock and cut out; discard the window cutout. Use the stylus to score the piece along the dashed lines; fold along the scored lines. Tape the box together, overlapping the grey areas where indicated on the pattern.*
2. Place wrapped cookies in the box and fold down the top. Tie a ribbon around the box. Add a seasonal message to a layered cardstock tag and tie to the bow with floss.

Square Gift Box
(also shown on page 53)
- transfer paper
- solid and patterned cardstock
- ¹/₄" hole punch
- stylus or bone folder
- double-sided tape
- ribbon
- rub-on letters
- photo corners
- snowflake punch
- acrylic gems
- craft glue

1. Enlarge the pattern on page 156 to 150%. *Transfer (page 137) the pattern to cardstock twice and cut out. Use the stylus to score the box pieces along the dashed lines; fold along the scored lines. Tape the box pieces together, overlapping the grey areas where indicated on the pattern.*
2. Place the gift in the box and tuck in the sides. Tie a ribbon through the punched holes. Use rub-on letters to personalize a layered cardstock tag. Adhere the tag and photo corners to the box. Glue punched snowflakes and gems to the box.

Triangular Gift Box

(also shown on page 53)
- transfer paper
- patterned cardstock
- stylus or bone folder
- double-sided tape
- alphabet stickers
- ribbon
- decorative brad

1. Enlarge the pattern on page 151 to 230%. *Transfer* (page 137) the pattern to cardstock and cut out. Use the stylus to score the piece along the dashed lines; fold along the scored lines. Tape the long flap to the wrong side of the opposite long edge, forming a triangular tube.

2. Place the gift in the box and tuck in the ends (tape the ends if desired). Add a seasonal message to a layered cardstock tag. Adhere the tag to the box and embellish with ribbon and a decorative brad.

Menswear Gift Sacks

(also shown on page 53)

These versatile gift sacks vary just a bit in construction. Choose a square-corner bag with a simple drawstring, a boxed-corner bag with a double-ended drawstring or a softly gathered-corner bag with a ruffled casing for the drawstring. Use a $1/2$" seam allowance for all sewing unless otherwise indicated.

Boxed-Corner Bag

- 15"x28" piece of menswear fabric
- 2 yards of $7/8$"w ribbon
- $5^1/2$"x$6^1/2$" wool scrap for pocket
- felt scraps
- fabric glue
- embroidery floss
- black size 10 sew-on snap for eyes
- seasonal message stamp and ink pad

1. Matching short ends and right sides, fold the fabric piece in half. Sew the side seams. Flatten and center each side seam against the bottom of the bag; sew across each corner $1^1/4$" from the point (Fig. 1). Turn the sack right side out and press the top edge $1/4$", then $1^1/4$" to the inside. Sew along the bottom folded edge and $1/4$" from the top folded edge.

Fig. 1

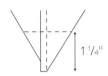

$1^1/4$"

2. Carefully remove the stitching from both side seams in the casing area. Cut the ribbon in half and thread 1 length through the front casing and 1 length through the back casing; knot the ends together and trim.

3. Enlarge the patterns (page 152) to 200%. Using the enlarged patterns, cut the snowman appliqué pieces. Press all pocket piece edges $1/4$" to the wrong side. Glue the appliqués to the pocket. Use floss to work *Blanket Stitches* (page 138) around the snowman, *French Knots* for his mouth, *Straight Stitches* for the mouth corner and a *French Knot* and *Straight Stitch* snowflake in the pocket corner. Sew on the snap eyes. Stamp a corner with the holiday message. Attach the pocket to the bag with floss

Blanket Stitches. For the scarf, cut $3/4$"x$6^1/2$" and $3/4$"x3" felt pieces. Fringe the ends of the $6^1/2$" length. Fold and glue the scarf to the snowman.

Square-Corner Bag

- 20"x31" piece of menswear fabric
- $1^3/4$ yards of 1"w ribbon
- 6"x$7^3/4$" wool scrap for pocket
- felted wool scrap
- decorative brad
- embroidery floss

1. Matching short ends and right sides, fold the fabric piece in half. Sew the side seams. Turn the sack right side out and press the top edge $1/4$", then $1^1/4$" to the inside. Sew along the bottom folded edge.

2. Carefully remove the stitching from one side seam in the casing area. Thread the ribbon through the casing, knot the ends together and trim.

3. Press all pocket piece edges $1/4$" to the wrong side. Use floss to work *Stem Stitches* (page 139) to attach a felted wool monogram (pick a favorite font from your computer) to the pocket. Add a small felted wool circle and a decorative brad to the corner. Attach the pocket to the bag with *Blanket Stitches*.

Gathered-Corner Bag

- 16"x29" piece of menswear fabric
- 1¼ yards of 1"w ribbon for drawstring
- felt scrap
- 1¾ yards of 1"w ribbon for flower
- fabric glue
- 4"x4" fabric scrap for pocket
- 1"w ribbon scraps for leaves and tag
- seasonal message stamp and ink pad
- acrylic gem brad
- embroidery floss

1. Matching short ends and right sides, fold the fabric piece in half. Sew the side seams. For the gathered corners, baste diagonally across each bottom corner. Pull basting threads tight and securely knot the thread ends. Turn the sack right side out and press the top edge ¼", then 2¼" to the inside. Sew along the bottom folded edge and 1¼" from the top folded edge.
2. Carefully remove the stitching from one side seam in the casing area. Thread the ribbon through the casing and trim the ends.
3. Cut a 2¾" diameter felt circle. Twist and glue one end of the flower ribbon to the felt circle center. Continue twisting and gluing in a spiral to cover the circle; trim as needed.

4. Press all pocket piece edges ¼" to the wrong side. Glue the flower, folded ribbon leaves and the ribbon tag to the pocket piece. Stamp the ribbon tag and add the brad. Use floss to work *Running Stitches* (page 139) along the pocket top edge and *Blanket Stitches* to attach the pocket to the bag.

Snow Day Pillow

(also shown on page 55)
- 16" pillow form
- 17"x17" fabric square for pillow back
- 17"x17" felted wool square for pillow front
- 12"x12" felt square for "snow"
- felt and felted wool scraps for appliqués
- tissue paper
- embroidery floss
- craft glue

Read Embroidery Stitches, pages 138-139, before beginning. Use 2 strands of floss.

1. Enlarge the pattern (page 153) to 143%. Use the enlarged pattern and *transfer* (page 137) the design to the 12"x12" felt square. Also use the pattern to make the boy, girl and snowman appliqué pieces from scraps. Pin the appliqué pieces to the felt square.

2. Referring to the key, use 2 strands of floss to embroider the design on the square and to attach all the appliqué pieces (except the children's hats and shoes) with *Blanket Stitch, Stem Stitch* and *Straight Stitch*. Fill in the words with *Stem Stitches.* Embroider the details. For the girl's hair, cut 1" lengths of floss, separate the strands and glue in place. Repeat for the boy's hair. Trim the hair to the desired lengths. Use *Straight Stitch* to attach the hats and shoes; add the embroidered hat details.
3. Zigzag the embroidered felt square to the center of the 17"x17" felted wool square.
4. Matching right sides and leaving an opening for turning, use a ½" seam allowance to sew the 17"x17" fabric squares together. Turn right side out, insert the pillow form and sew the opening closed.

Tractor Hat

(continued from page 56)
Read Embroidery Stitches, pages 138-139, before beginning. Use 3 strands of floss.

1. Fuse web to the wrong side of the appliqué fabric scraps.

2. Enlarge the patterns (page 154) to 200%. Using the enlarged tractor pattern, cut fabric scrap appliqués. Fuse, then use nylon thread to zigzag the appliqués to the felt piece. Embroider the design using *Stem Stitch*, *Straight Stitch* and *French Knots*. Sew the snap pieces to the tractor wheels. Trim the felt about ¹/₈" from the design. Whipstitch the appliqué to the hat.

3. Make a 2" pom-pom (page 140) and sew to the hat top.

4. For ear flap strings, crochet two 10" long chains, leaving long yarn tails at the beginnings. Using the enlarged ear flap pattern, cut 2 ear flaps and 2 lining pieces. Pin the finishing ends of the chains to the center of the curved edges of the ear flaps. Matching right sides, using a ¹/₄" seam allowance and leaving the straight edge open, sew each ear flap to a lining piece, catching the chain end in the stitching. Clip the curves, turn right side out and press. Turn the raw edges ¹/₄" to the inside and slipstitch the opening closed. Whipstitch the flaps to the inside of the hat.

Mitten Puppet
(also shown on page 56)
- knit mitten
- paper-backed fusible web
- fabric and felt scraps
- ¹/₂" dia. pom-pom
- two ⁵/₈" dia. buttons

1. Fuse web to the wrong side of the fabric scraps.

2. Enlarge the patterns (page 157) to 200%. Using the enlarged patterns, cut the tongue and ears from the fabric scraps and the eyes, eyelashes and ridge plates from the felt scraps. Fuse the tongue and ears to coordinating felt scraps and trim ¹/₈" from fabric.

3. Place the mitten on your hand and use pins to mark the positions of the tongue, nose, eyes, ears, and the ridge plates. Sew the tongue, pom-pom nose, ears (folding in half at the straight edge) and ridge plates to the mitten. For the eyes, layer the eyelashes, eyes, and buttons and sew onto the mitten, leaving the eyelashes free at the top.

Vintage Fabric Scarf
(also shown on page 57)
- ³/₄ yard vintage fabric for scarf
- assorted fabric scraps for mini bundle fringe
- polyester fiberfill
- medium weight yarn [1.75 ounces, 98 yards (50 grams, 90 meters)]
- crochet hook, size F (3.75 mm) **or** size needed for gauge
  Gauge Swatch:
  5" (12.5 cm) wide
  Work same as Rows 1-3.

Read Crochet on page 140 before beginning. Always match right sides and use a ¹/₂" seam allowance when sewing.

1. Cut four 6"x40" pieces of fabric. Sew 2 fabric pieces together along one short end. Repeat with the remaining fabric pieces. Matching the right sides and leaving an opening for turning, sew the fabric pieces together on all sides. Clip the corners, turn right side out and press. Sew the opening closed.

2. For the crocheted edgings, work 2 pieces as follows:
  Ch 20.
  Row 1: Sc in second ch from hook and in each ch across: 19 sc.
  Row 2: Ch 1, turn; sc in each sc across.
  Row 3: Ch 1, turn; sc in each sc across.
  Row 4: Ch 1, turn; sc in first sc, ★ ch 6, skip 2 sc, sc in next sc; repeat from ★ to end of row; finish off.

3. For each fabric bundle, cut a 2¹/₂" fabric circle. Work *Running Stitches* (page 139) ¹/₄" from the edge and tightly gather the bundle, placing a bit of fiberfill in the center. Wrap the bundle top with the thread and securely knot.

4. Sew the edgings to the scarf ends. Sew the fabric bundles to the edging loops.

Big, Beautiful Tote
(continued from page 58)

3. From each fabric for stripes, cut six 2"x7" fabric strips. Arranging the fabrics in random order and offsetting the strips by 1", use a ¹/₄" seam allowance to sew the long edges of 4 fabric strips together (Fig. 1). Repeat to make 17 more strip sets.

Fig. 1

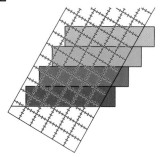

4. Align the 60° line on the rotary ruler with the bottom edge of one strip set and trim the fabric right edge with the rotary cutter (Fig. 2).

Fig. 2

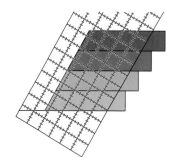

5. Rotate the trimmed strip set so that the trimmed edge is on the left. Aligning the 60° line on the ruler with the bottom edge again, place the ruler on the strip set so that the 4¹/₄" mark on the ruler is aligned with the trimmed edge (Fig. 3). Cut on the right side on the ruler. Repeat Steps 4 and 5 with the remaining strip sets.

Fig. 3

6. Using a ¹/₄" seam allowance, sew 3 strip sets together (Fig. 4). Repeat to make 6 striped bands.

7. For the front striped panel, refer to Fig. 5 and sew 3 striped bands together, slightly offsetting the seams. Trim the striped panel to 19"w. Repeat for the back striped panel.

Fig. 4

Fig. 5

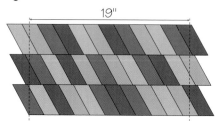

8. Mark the brown bottom pieces at 1⁵/₈" and 2³/₄" from the top (Fig. 6). Fold the fabric along these marks and topstitch close to the fold, creating pintucks.

Fig. 6

9. For the tote front, sew a brown top, the front striped panel and a brown bottom together (Fig. 7). Repeat for the tote back with the back striped panel.

Fig. 7

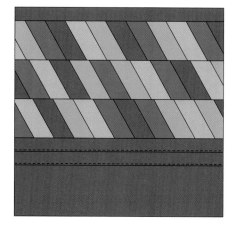

10. Sew the tote front and back together along the sides and bottom. Flatten and match the side seams to the bottom seam and sew across each corner 2¹/₄" from the point (Fig. 8). Turn right side out.

Fig. 8

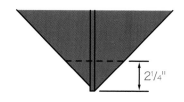

11. For each strap, press the long edges $1/2$" to the wrong side. Matching the wrong sides, fold the strap in half lengthwise and press; topstitch along both long edges. Matchng the raw edges and leaving $4^1/2$" between the strap ends, center and pin the straps on the tote front and back.

12. Sew the remaining brown top pieces to the larger lining pieces. Repeat Step 10 with the larger lining pieces, leaving an opening along the bottom for turning. Do not turn the lining right side out.

13. Matching the right sides, insert the tote in the lining. Sew the tote and lining together along the top edge. Turn right side out and sew the opening closed. Tuck the lining in the tote. Topstitch close to the seam between the top brown pieces and the striped panels of the tote.

14. Sew the remaining lining pieces together along the long edges and one short end. Turn right side out and insert the cardboard. Fold the fabric raw edges to the inside and sew the opening closed. Insert the covered cardboard in the tote. Slipstitch to the lining if desired.

Yo-Yo Sewing Kit
(continued from page 62)
2. Center and fuse the interfacing to the wrong side of the lining fabric. Cut a $2^3/4$"x2" rectangle and two $3/4$" diameter circles from the

felt. Referring to Fig. 1, use *Running Stitches* (page 139) to sew one long edge of the felt rectangle to the lining fabric. Use long *Straight Stitches* to sew a felt circle and one snap piece near the top.

Fig. 1

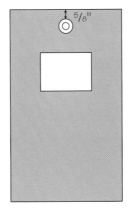

3. Sew the remaining felt circle and snap piece to the right side of the lining fabric rectangle (Fig. 2).

Fig. 2

4. Matching the right sides, using a $1/2$" seam allowance and leaving an opening for turning, sew the lining and rectangle together. Clip the corners, turn right side out and press. Sew the opening closed.

5. Slipstitch the lined fabric piece to the yo-yo's, leaving about $2^1/4$" of each yo-yo unstitched.

Coiled Rag Basket
(also shown on page 65)
- $3/16$" dia. poly-reinforced cotton clothesline (two 50-foot packages)
- 2 yards total of assorted fabrics (we used 8 different fabrics)
- 2 large spools of sewing thread (we used white for a "rag" look)
- rotary cutter, rotary ruler and cutting mat
- size 90/14 sharp sewing machine needle

1. Use the rotary cutter, ruler and mat to cut fabrics into $1/2$" wide strips, cutting selvage to selvage.

2. Wrap one clothesline cord end with a fabric strip and stitch, catching the cord in the stitching (Fig. 1).

Fig. 1

3. Wrap the fabric strip around the cord, angling the fabric as you wrap toward your body. When you get to the end of the fabric strip, pin the loose fabric end in place.

4. Fold about 6" of the cord down to the left and place the fold under the presser foot. Using a wide stitch width and short stitch length, zigzag the folded area (Fig. 2).

Fig. 2

5. When you reach the end of the folded cord, stop with the needle in the cord, pivot the work and continue zigzagging the cord together (Fig. 3).

Fig. 3

6. To add a new fabric strip, slip the new strip between the cord and the old strip (Fig. 4); continue wrapping, zigzagging and pivoting until the base is about 7½"x12½".

Fig. 4

132

7. To add height to the basket, hold the base at an angle to the sewing machine (Fig. 5). Continue wrapping and zigzagging around the base until the basket is about 5½" high.

Fig. 5

8. Cut the cord and fabric strip, leaving a 4" length of fabric. Wrap the cord end with the fabric, zigzag over the cord end, backstitch, and trim the excess fabric.

Cake Box
(also shown on page 67)
- craft knife and cutting mat
- 10"x10"x5" one-piece fold-out cake box
- double-sided tape
- acetate sheet
- patterned cardstock
- low-temp glue gun
- three ½" dia. buttons
- food tissue paper
- Blueberry Cream Coffee Cake (page 67)
- 2¾ yards of ¼"w gingham ribbon

1. Enlarge the window pattern (page 144) to 200% and the holly leaf pattern from the Mini Pennant Swag (page 141) to 292%. Using the window pattern, cut the shape from the center of the box lid. Tape acetate to the inside lid.
2. Cut 4 cardstock leaves; fold 2 in half lengthwise. Glue the crease of each folded leaf to a flat leaf.
3. For each berry, accordion-fold a ¾"x12" cardstock strip. Glue the ends of the strip together and add a button to the center.
4. Line the box with tissue paper and place the cake inside. Glue the leaves and berries to ribbon tied around the box.

Chip & Dip Mix Container
(also shown on page 68)
- large clear acrylic container with latched lid (ours is 9"hx5" dia.)
- Santa's Zesty Mix (page 68) in a plastic zipping bag (ours is 3"x4½") and Baked Pita Chips (page 68)
- cardstock
- scallop-edged scissors
- double-sided tape
- 1"w grosgrain ribbon
- alphabet stamps with red and black ink pads
- hole punch
- ¼"w ribbon

1. Tape a scalloped cardstock circle to the lid of the pita chip-filled container. Tie 1"w ribbon around the lid.

2. For the dip mix, cut a cardstock rectangle slightly larger than the mix bag, scalloping the ends. Fold in half. Tape a stamped cardstock label to the front. Place the folded cardstock over the bag and punch a hole through all layers (above the bag "zipper"). Tie together with ¼"w ribbon.

Macaroons 4 U! Box

(also shown on page 68)
- plastic-wrapped Cocoa-Cherry Macaroons (page 68)
- gift box (ours measures 6"wx4½"hx4½"d)
- pinking shears
- ⅛ yard each of 2 coordinating fabrics
- contrasting thread
- ½"w ribbon
- rub-on letters and number 4
- purchased tag

1. Place macaroons in the box.

2. Measure around the box and add 8". Use pinking shears to cut one 4"w and one 2½"w fabric strip this length (we cut ours 26" long).

3. To make the fabric band, layer the strips and follow Fig. 1 to press pleats at the center of the strips. Use contrasting thread to topstitch the strips together through the center. Matching right sides and short ends, sew the ends together to fit around the box. Turn right side out and slip the band over the box.

Fig. 1

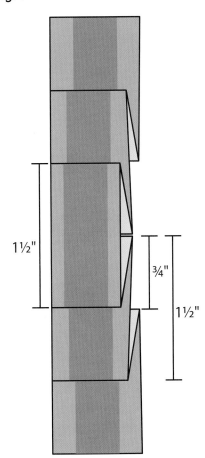

1½"

¾"

1½"

4. Tie ribbon around the box. Add the rub-on message to the tag and secure it to the bow.

Card

(also shown on page 69)
- double-sided cardstock
- cream and dark brown cardstock
- pinking shears
- glue stick
- three ¾" dia. self-covered buttons
- red fabric scraps
- wire cutters
- adhesive foam dots
- green felt scrap
- craft knife and cutting mat
- Rustic Apple Tart (page 69)

1. For the gift card, match short ends and fold a 5¼"x10½" cardstock piece in half.

2. Print the card label on cream cardstock; cut out with pinking shears. Glue the label to the card front.

3. Cover the buttons; remove the shanks with wire cutters. Adhere to the card front with foam dots. Cut felt leaves and dark brown cardstock stems. Glue to the card front above the "apple" buttons.

4. Print the recipe or a seasonal message on cardstock and trim to a 4"x4" square. Place the square inside the card, using the craft knife to cut slits for the corners to slip into. Place the tart on a pretty plate and give with the card.

Gift Box

(also shown on page 71)
- acrylic container with scoop
  (our container is 4"wx3"dx5"h)
- solid and patterned cardstock
- 1½" dia. scalloped circle punch
- double-sided tape
- bagged A Merry Mix (page 71)
- 1"w grosgrain ribbon
- tracing paper
- flocking kit (including adhesive
  and colored flocking fibers)
- scrapbooking mini game piece
  with letter "A"
- rub-on letters
- adhesive foam dots

1. Line the inside lower half of
the container with a patterned
cardstock strip; overlap and tape
the ends together. Place the
bagged mix inside, then tie ribbon
around the container.
2. Using the pattern on page 143,
cut a cardstock sprig. Cut 1 circle
each from cardstock: 2½", 2¼",
2" and 1". Punch a scalloped circle.
Add flocked dots around the 1"
circle and glue to the scalloped
flower. Glue the game piece in
place.

3. Flock the berries, then glue the
sprig to the 2" circle. Add rub-ons
and back with the 2½" circle. Glue
the scalloped circle to the layered
circles.
4. Tape the 2½" circle to the
container (behind the ribbon).
Adhere the layered pieces to the
2½" circle with foam dots.

Cheese Ball Box

(also shown on page 71)
- transfer paper
- double-sided patterned
  cardstock
- double-sided tape
- acetate sheet
- craft glue
- glitter
- scrapbook paper
- photo corners
- 2 brads
- ribbon scrap
- rub-on letters
- large paper muffin cup
- plastic-wrapped Pineapple &
  Nut Cheese Ball (page 71)
- ¾ yard of rickrack
- vintage cheese spreader

1. Enlarge the box patterns
(page 155) to 200%. Transfer the
patterns to cardstock; cut out
along the solid lines, discarding the
window. Tape acetate to the wrong
side of the window opening. Accent
the cardstock design with glitter
2. Overlap and tape the top to the
box along the grey area. Score,
then fold the box along the dashed
lines and tape together.
3. Glue a scrapbook paper house
design to the lid, adding photo
corners at the top. Use brads
to attach a ribbon with a rub-on
message. Mount a printed label on
a slightly larger scrapbook paper
piece and tape to the lid.
4. Place the muffin cup and cheese
ball in the box. Wrap rickrack
around the box, securing the
spreader at the side.

Scone Cozy

(also shown on page 72)
- cotton batting circles (one 13"
  and one 10" dia.)
- cozy fabric circles (two 13" and
  one 10" dia.)
- 6 fabric scraps for pockets
- scallop-edged fabric scissors
- clear nylon thread
- 1½" dia. button
- embellished cardstock tag (we
  used alphabet stamps, ink
  pad, chipboard label holder,
  decorative brads, embroidery
  floss and a button)
- wrapped Cranberry Scones
  (page 72)

Match wrong sides of fabric unless otherwise noted.

1. Sandwich the large batting circle between the large fabric circles. Topstitch all layers together 1/2" from the outer edge.

2. Enlarge the pattern (page 143) to 200%. Use the enlarged pattern to cut 6 fabric pockets with scallop-edged scissors. Center the small batting circle on the wrong side of the small fabric circle. Place the pocket pieces on the batting circle, matching the outer edges (the pocket pieces will overlap). Zigzag the overlaps in place; then, topstitch 1/2" from the outer edge of the circle.

3. Scallop the edges of both circles. Center the small circle on the large one. Pin at the seams so each pocket bulges enough for a scone to fit inside (the center will buckle a bit). Using clear thread, stitch over each seam from the outer edge to 1" from the center.

4. Sew the button and embellished tag to the center. Place a scone in each pocket.

Potholder
(also shown on page 73)
- vintage linens (we used napkins with red and green corner motifs)
- batting
- backing fabric (we used red & white ticking)
- red and green embroidery floss
- jumbo green rickrack
- baby red rickrack

Use a 1/2" seam allowance unless otherwise noted.

1. For each potholder, cut an 8" square each from linen, batting and backing fabric.

2. Using 6 strands of floss, add *French Knots* (page 139) and *Stem Stitches* to the motifs. Zigzag the rickrack lengths to the fabric.

3. Match right sides and layer the backing, linen and batting pieces. Leaving an opening for turning, sew the layers together. Turn right side out and sew the opening closed.

Candy Glass
(also shown on page 73)
- Chocolate Peanut Clusters (page 73)
- vintage Christmas drinking glass
- clear cellophane
- two 8" lengths of 1/4"w gingham ribbon
- assorted red buttons
- patterned cardstock
- hot glue gun
- "JOY" rub-on
- black fine-point permanent pen

---

1. Line the glass with cellophane and add a stack of peanut clusters. Tie closed with a ribbon length.

2. Thread a button to the center of the remaining ribbon. Stack and hot glue buttons around the edge of a 2 1/2" diameter cardstock circle. Glue the ribbon-threaded button to the top. Apply the rub-on to the center and write "peanut" and "clusters" above and below "JOY."

3. Tie on the tag and trim the cellophane.

Pie Basket
(also shown on page 75)
- double-lidded picnic basket (our 7"wx12"lx4"h basket holds two 4 1/2" dia. pie pans)
- liner fabric
- 1"w grosgrain ribbon (we used 2 1/8 yards)
- ball fringe (we used 1 1/8 yards)
- 2 Mock Cherry Pies (page 75)
- solid and patterned cardstock
- double-sided tape
- scallop-edged scissors
- letter stickers ("pie" and "cherry")
- paper flower embellishment
- adhesive foam dots
- rub-on letters
- purchased mini tag
- brown scrapbooking chalk
- black fine-point permanent pen
- hole punch
- brad
- assorted ribbons

When sewing, always match right sides and use a ¼" seam allowance.

1. For the liner bottom, measure the inside length and width of the basket; add ½" to each measurement. Cut a fabric piece the determined size.

2. For the liner sides, measure around the outer basket rim; measure the height of the basket and add the amount of overhang you want on the side. Add ½" to each measurement. Cut a fabric piece the determined measurements.

3. Matching the short ends, sew the liner side piece together, forming a ring. Matching the seam to a corner, sew the liner side to the liner bottom, pleating the excess side fabric as necessary.

4. To trim the liner around the handles, place the liner in the basket and arrange the overhang as evenly as possible on all sides. Cut a rectangle from each side edge ¼" smaller than the desired finished notch (Fig. 1). Clip the corners; then, turn and sew the notched edges ¼" to the wrong side.

Fig. 1

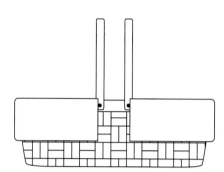

5. Measure around the basket rim and cut 2 pieces of 1"w ribbon this length. Cut 2 pieces of ball fringe half this length. Center and pin the ball fringe on each ribbon length, turning the short ball fringe ends ½" to the wrong side. Covering the raw edges, center and sew the trims on the right side of the liner, leaving the ribbon ends loose for ties. Place the liner and pies in the basket. Tie the ribbon ends.

6. For the label, cut and layer 3 cardstock circles, scalloping the largest circle. Adhere "Pie" to the label and "cherry" on top. Use foam dots to adhere the paper flower to the label. Add rub-on letters to spell "mock" on the mini tag; adhere to the label with foam dots. Chalk the label and tag edges and add pen-line dashes and dots just for fun! Attach the brad to the label and loop the mini tag over the brad. Tie the label to the basket with colorful ribbons.

General Instructions

Making Patterns

When the entire pattern is shown, place tracing or tissue paper over the pattern and draw over the lines. For a more durable pattern, use a permanent marker to draw over the pattern on stencil plastic.

When only half of the pattern is shown (indicated by a solid gold line on the pattern), fold the tracing paper in half. Place the fold along the solid gold line and trace the pattern half. Turn the folded paper over and draw over the traced lines on the remaining side. Unfold the pattern and cut it out.

Sizing Patterns

1. To change the size of the pattern, divide the desired height or width of the pattern (whichever is greater) by the actual height or width of the pattern. Multiply the result by 100 and photocopy the pattern at this percentage.

For example: You want your pattern to be 8"h, but the pattern on the page is 6"h. So 8÷6=1.33x100=133%. Copy the pattern at 133%.

2. If your copier doesn't enlarge to the size you need, enlarge the pattern to the maximum percentage on the copier. Then repeat step 1, dividing the desired size by the size of the enlarged pattern. Multiply this result by 100 and photocopy the enlarged pattern at the new percentage.

For very large projects, you'll need to enlarge the design in sections onto separate sheets of paper. Repeat as needed to reach the desired size and tape the pattern pieces together.

Transferring Patterns To Fabrics

Trace the pattern onto tissue paper. Pin the tissue paper to the felt or fabric and stitch through the paper. Carefully tear the tissue paper away.

Transferring Patterns To Cardstock Or Other Materials

Trace the paper onto tracing paper. Place the pattern on the cardstock (or whatever material you are transferring to) and use a pencil to lightly draw around the pattern. For pattern details, slip transfer paper between the pattern and the cardstock and draw over the detail lines.

Cutting a Stencil

Enlarge the pattern if necessary. Using a fine-point permanent marker, trace the pattern onto stencil plastic or mylar. Carefully cut the plastic with scissors or a craft knife, making sure all edges are smooth.

Making a Fabric Circle

Matching right sides, fold the fabric square in half from top to bottom and again from left to right. Tie one end of a length of string to a water-soluble marking pen; insert a thumbtack through the string at the length indicated in the project instructions. Insert the thumbtack through the folded corner of the fabric. Holding the tack in place and keeping the string taut, mark the cutting line (Fig. 1).

Fig. 1

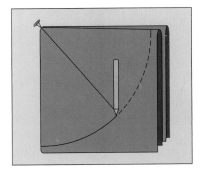

Making and Using Wood Letter Stamps

- craft foam
- craft knife and cutting mat
- scrap wood pieces
- craft glue
- masking tape
- solvent-based permanent ink pad, such as StazOn®

Print 2 copies of the letters or word from your computer in the desired sizes and fonts. Using the printouts as patterns, cut out letters or word from craft foam (Fig. 2, page 138).

Fig. 2

Glue letters or word, *wrong side up*, to scrap wood pieces. Adhere masking tape along the edges of the letter or word and wrap the masking tape around to the wrong side of the stamping block (Fig. 3). This will make it easier to place the stamp right where you want it.

Fig. 3

Before stamping, use the remaining paper printouts to arrange and space the letters. Use permanent ink to stamp letters or word on project.

Drybrushing

Without dipping in water, dip an old paintbrush in paint; wipe most of the paint off onto a dry paper towel. Lightly rub the brush across the surface and repeat for desired coverage.

Embroidery Stitches

Always come up at 1 and all odd numbers and go down at 2 and all even numbers unless otherwise indicated.

Backstitch

Bring the needle up at 1, go down at 2, come up at 3 and go down at 4 (Fig. 4).

Fig. 4

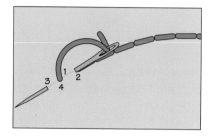

Blanket Stitch

Referring to Fig. 5, bring the needle up at 1. Keeping the thread below the point of the needle, go down at 2 and come up at 3. Continue working as shown in Fig. 6.

Fig. 5

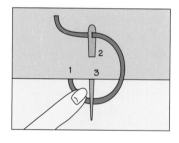

Fig. 6

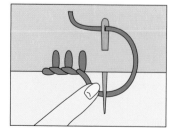

Bullion Knot

Referring to Fig. 7, bring the needle up at 1 and take the needle down at 2 (this is the distance the knot will cover); come up at 1 again and wrap the yarn around the needle as many times as necessary to cover the distance between 1 and 2. Pull needle through wraps and adjust on the 1-2 loop (Figs. 8-9). Anchor the knot with a small straight stitch at 2 (Fig. 10).

Fig. 7

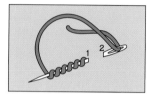

Fig. 8

Fig. 9

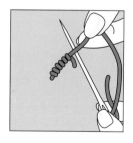

Fig. 10

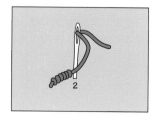

Chain Stitch

Referring to Fig. 11, bring the needle up at 1; take the needle down again at 1 to form a loop. Bring the needle up at 2; take the needle down again at 2 to form a second loop (Fig. 12). Continue making loops. Anchor the last chain with a small straight stitch (Fig. 13).

Fig. 11

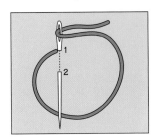

Fig. 12

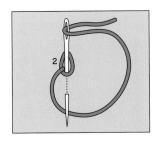

Fig. 13

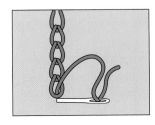

Couching Stitch

Referring to Fig. 14, lay the thread to be couched on the fabric; bring the needle up at 1 and go down at 2. Continue until entire thread length is couched.

Fig. 14

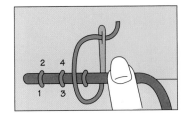

French Knot

Referring to Fig. 15, bring the needle up at 1. Wrap the floss once around the needle and insert the needle at 2, holding the floss end with non-stitching fingers. Tighten the knot; then, pull the needle through the fabric, holding the floss until it must be released. For a larger knot, use more strands; wrap only once.

Fig. 15

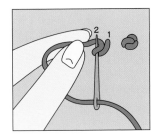

Lazy Daisy

Bring the needle up at 1; take the needle back down at 1 to form a loop and bring the needle up at 2. Keeping the loop below the point of the needle (Fig. 16), take the needle down at 3 to anchor the loop.

Fig. 16

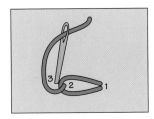

Running Stitch

Referring to Fig. 17, make a series of straight stitches with the stitch length equal to the space between stitches.

Fig. 17

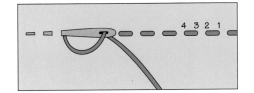

Stem Stitch

Referring to Fig. 18, come up at 1. Keeping the thread below the stitching line, go down at 2 and come up at 3. Go down at 4 and come up at 5.

Fig. 18

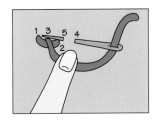

Straight Stitch

Referring to Fig. 19, come up at 1 and go down at 2.

Fig. 19

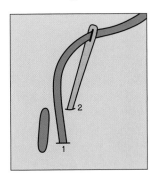

Needle Felting

Apply wool roving to a background fabric using a needle felting tool and mat (Fig. 20, page 140). Lightly punch the needles to interlock the fibers and join the pieces without sewing or gluing (Fig. 21, page 140). The brush-like mat allows the needles to easily pierce the fibers. We used the Clover Felting Needle Tool to make our projects—it has a locking plastic shield that provides protection from the sharp needles.

Fig. 20

Fig. 21

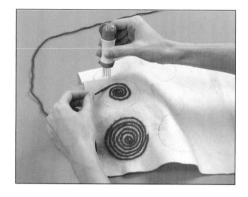

Pom-Poms

For a 2" diameter pom-pom, place an 8" piece of yarn along one long edge of a 1"x3" cardboard strip. Wrap yarn around and around the strip and yarn piece (Fig. 22) (the more you wrap, the fluffier the pom-pom). Tie the wound yarn together tightly with the 8" piece. Leaving the tie ends long to attach the pom-pom, cut the loops opposite the tie; then, fluff and trim the pom-pom into a smooth ball.

Fig. 22

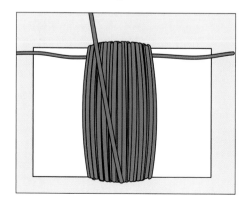

Making Yo-Yo's

To make each yo-yo, cut a circle as indicated in the project instructions, Press the circle edge ¼" to the wrong side and sew *Running Stitches* (page 139) around the edge with a doubled strand of thread. Pull the thread tightly to gather. Knot and trim the thread end. Flatten the yo-yo with the small opening at the center of the circle.

Shaping Eye Loops

Bend the end of a wire length or head pin to a 90° angle (Fig. 23). Repositioning the round nose pliers as needed, bend the wire end into a small loop (Fig. 24). Cut off any excess wire (Fig. 25). To open an eye loop, follow the instructions for opening a jump ring.

Fig. 23

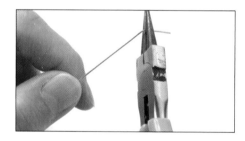

Fig. 24

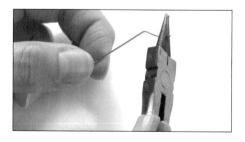

Fig. 25

Using Jump Rings

To open a jump ring without putting too much stress on the ring, use 2 pairs of needle-nose pliers to grasp each side of the ring near the opening. Pull one set of pliers toward you and push the other away to open the ring. Work the pliers in the opposite direction to close the ring.

Crochet
Abbreviations

ch(s)	chain(s)
cm	centimeters
mm	millimeters
sc	single crochet(s)
st(s)	stitch(es)

★ — work instructions following ★ as many **more** times as indicated in addition to the first time.

( ) or [ ] —contains explanatory remarks

colon (:) — the number given after a colon at the end of a row denotes the number of stitches you should have on that row.

GAUGE

Exact gauge is **essential** for proper fit. Before beginning your project, make a sample swatch in the yarn and hook specified. After completing the swatch, measure it, counting your stitches and rows or rounds carefully. If your swatch is larger or smaller than specified, make another, changing hook size to get the correct gauge. Keep trying until you find the size hook that will give you the specified gauge.

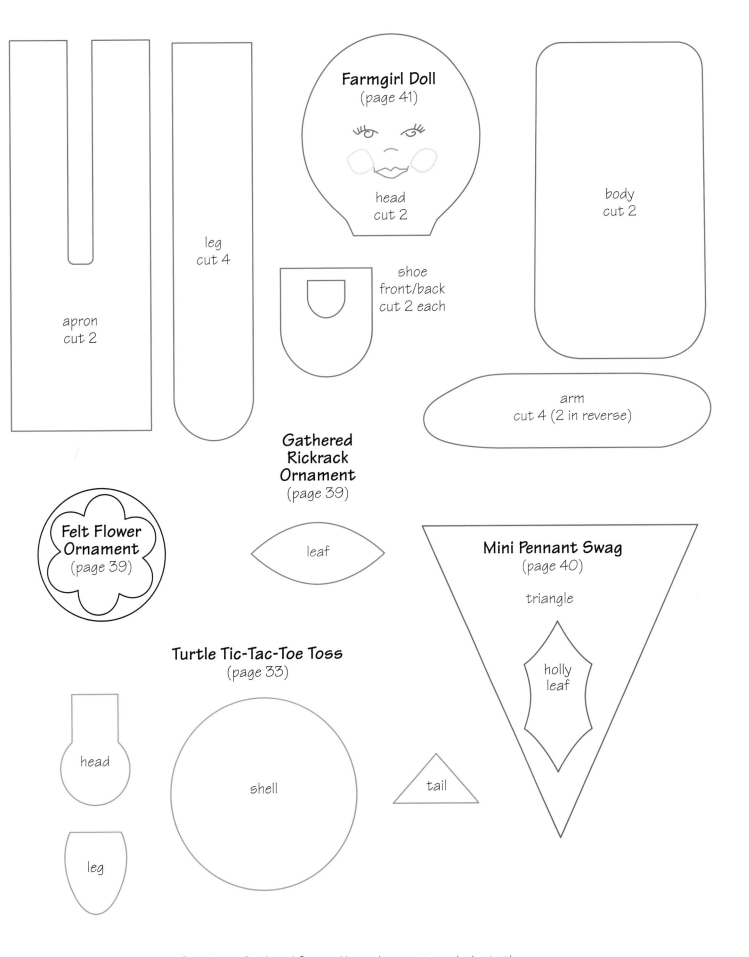

Farmgirl Doll
(page 41)

head
cut 2

body
cut 2

leg
cut 4

shoe
front/back
cut 2 each

arm
cut 4 (2 in reverse)

apron
cut 2

**Gathered
Rickrack
Ornament**
(page 39)

leaf

**Felt Flower
Ornament**
(page 39)

Mini Pennant Swag
(page 40)

triangle

holly
leaf

Turtle Tic-Tac-Toe Toss
(page 33)

head

shell

tail

leg

*Gooseberry Patch and Oxmoor House, Inc. grant permission to the owner
of this book to copy the designs in this book for personal use only.*

Horsie
(page 32)

body

ear

Bead Garland
(page 34)

Star Ornament/Tree Topper
(page 34)

large star

small star

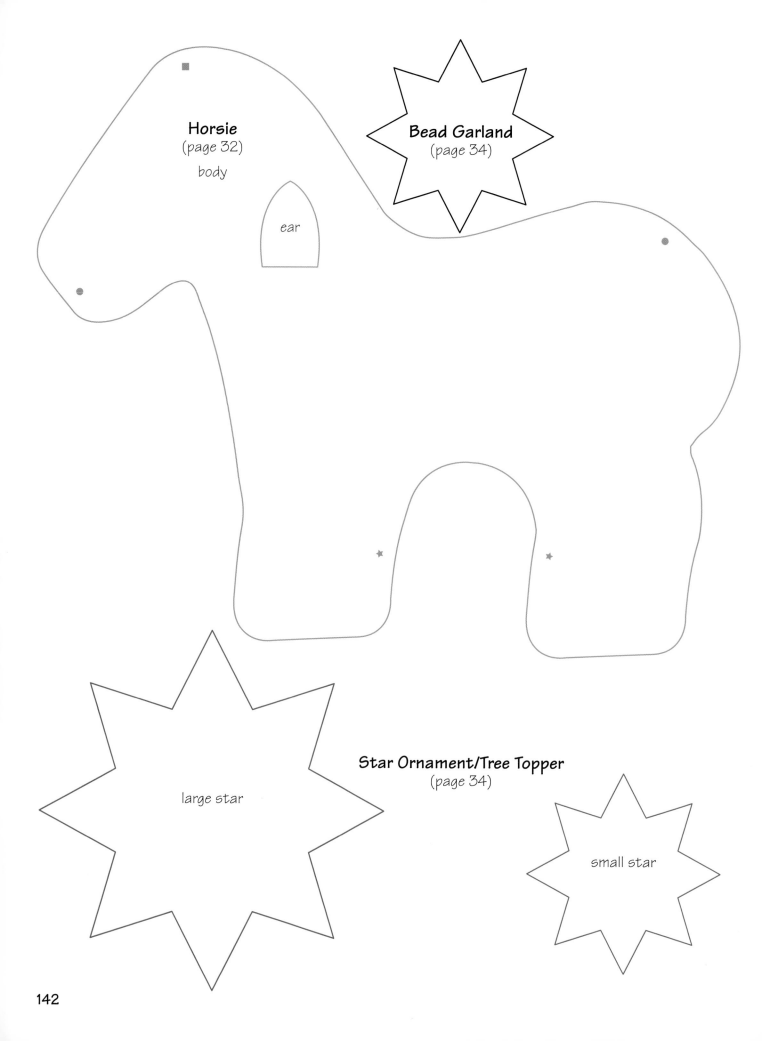

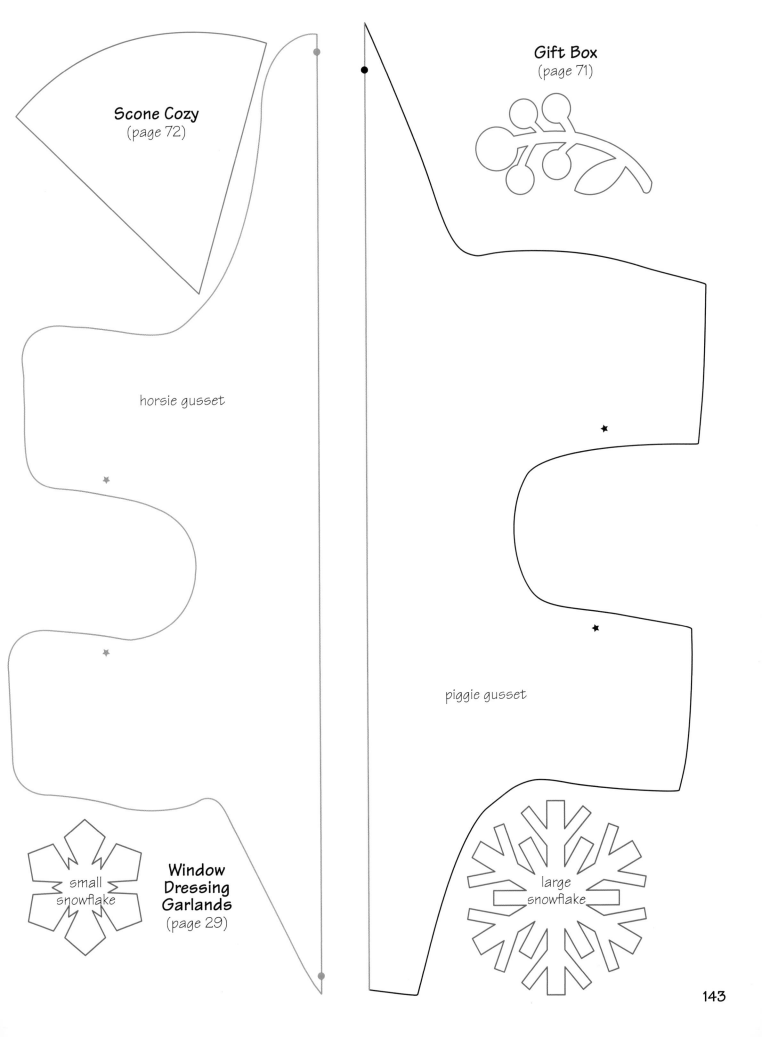

Scone Cozy
(page 72)

horsie gusset

Gift Box
(page 71)

piggie gusset

small
snowflake

**Window
Dressing
Garlands**
(page 29)

large
snowflake

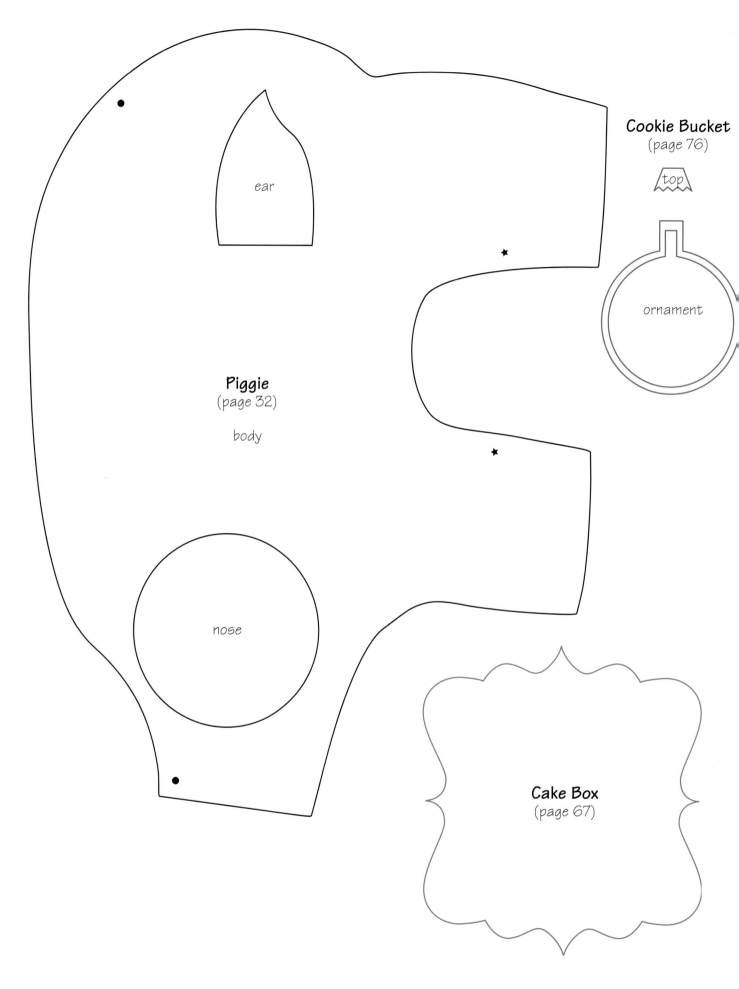

Cookie Bucket
(page 76)

top

ornament

Piggie
(page 32)

body

ear

nose

Cake Box
(page 67)

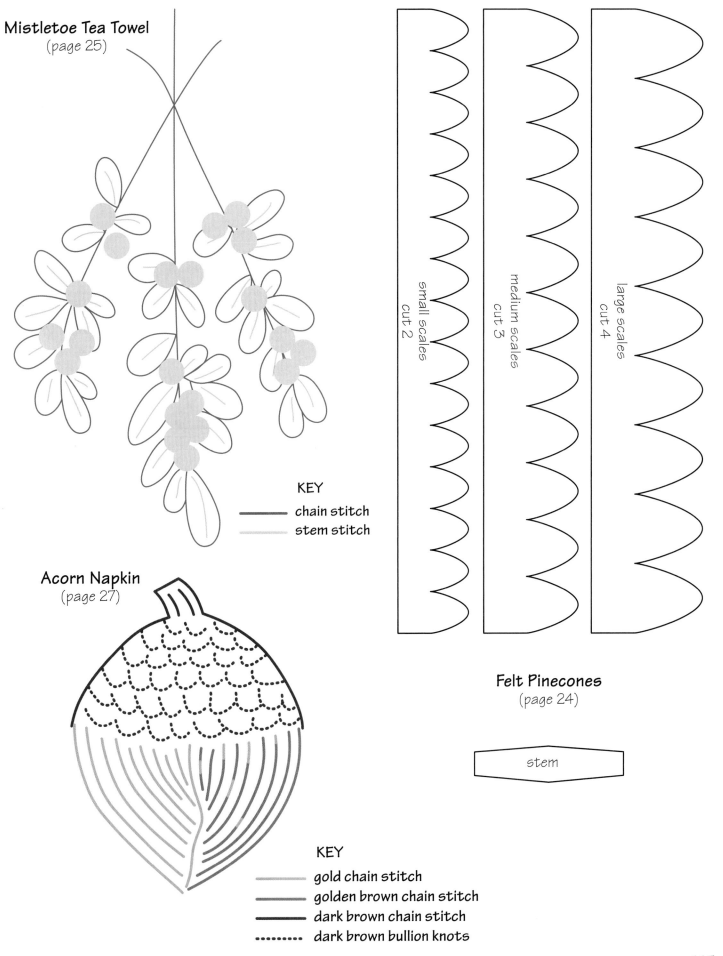

Mistletoe Tea Towel
(page 25)

KEY

—— chain stitch
—— stem stitch

Acorn Napkin
(page 27)

KEY

—— gold chain stitch
—— golden brown chain stitch
—— dark brown chain stitch
••••••• dark brown bullion knots

small scales
cut 2

medium scales
cut 3

large scales
cut 4

Felt Pinecones
(page 24)

stem

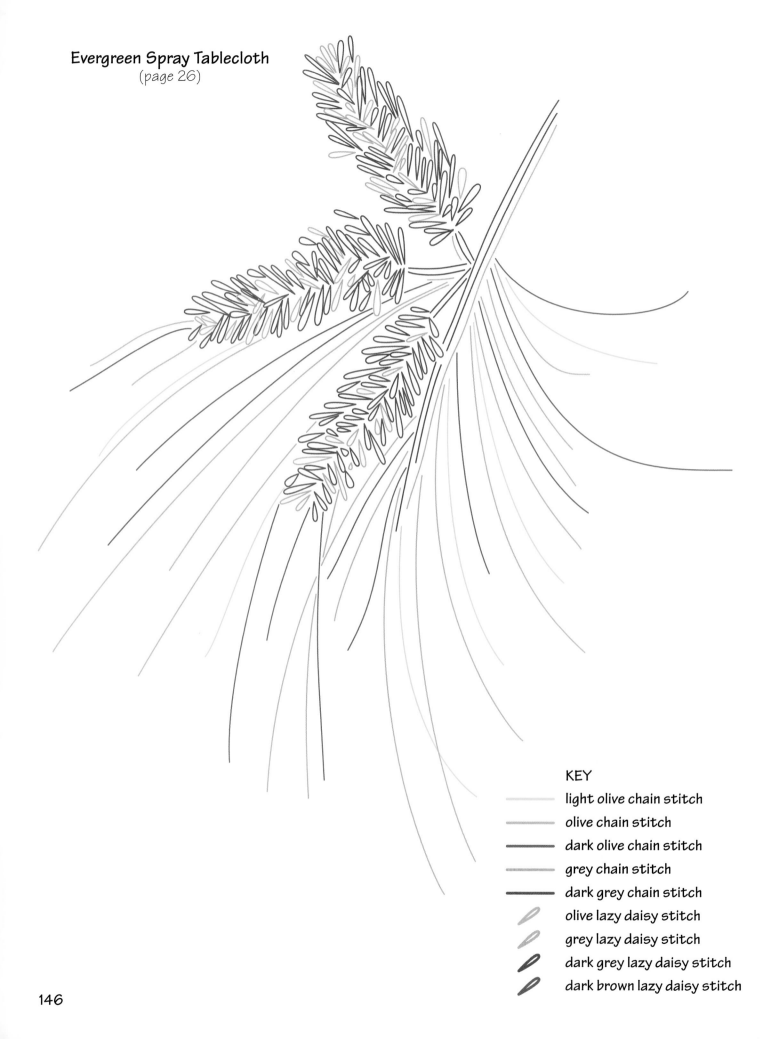

Evergreen Spray Tablecloth
(page 26)

KEY

light olive chain stitch

olive chain stitch

dark olive chain stitch

grey chain stitch

dark grey chain stitch

olive lazy daisy stitch

grey lazy daisy stitch

dark grey lazy daisy stitch

dark brown lazy daisy stitch

146

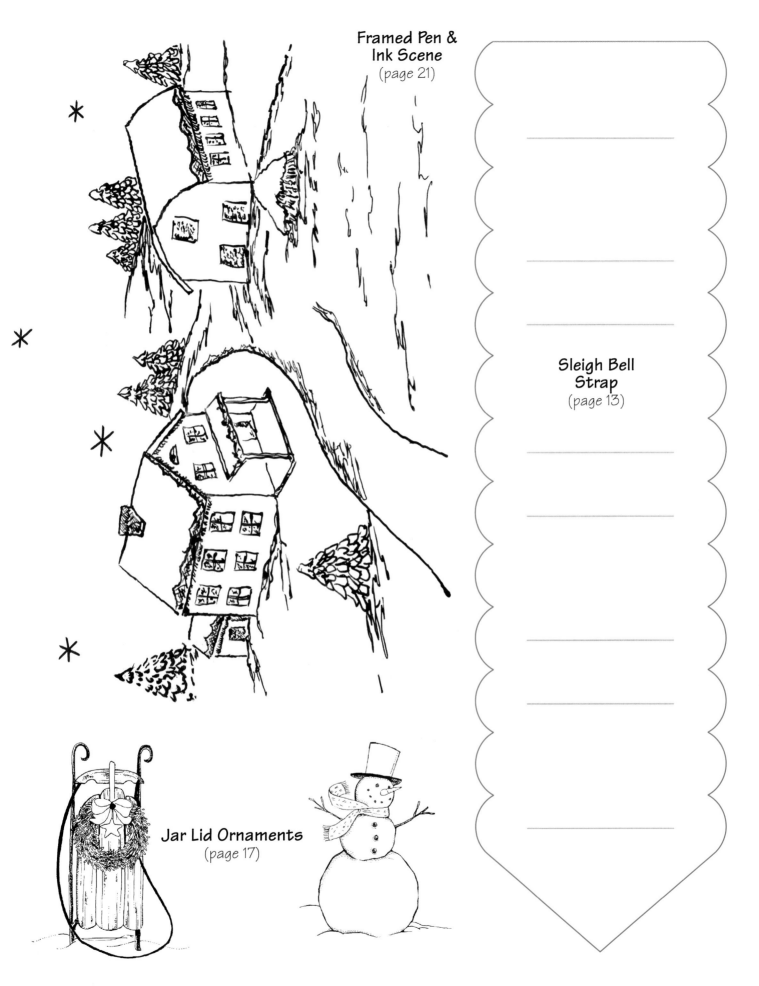

Framed Pen & Ink Scene
(page 21)

Sleigh Bell Strap
(page 13)

Jar Lid Ornaments
(page 17)

Lamp Post Banner
(page 11)

**Sweater
Tree Pillow**
(page 11)

tree

circle

trunk

wing/small leaf

Bird Stocking
(page 47)

bird

large leaf

Poinsettia Wreath
(page 51)

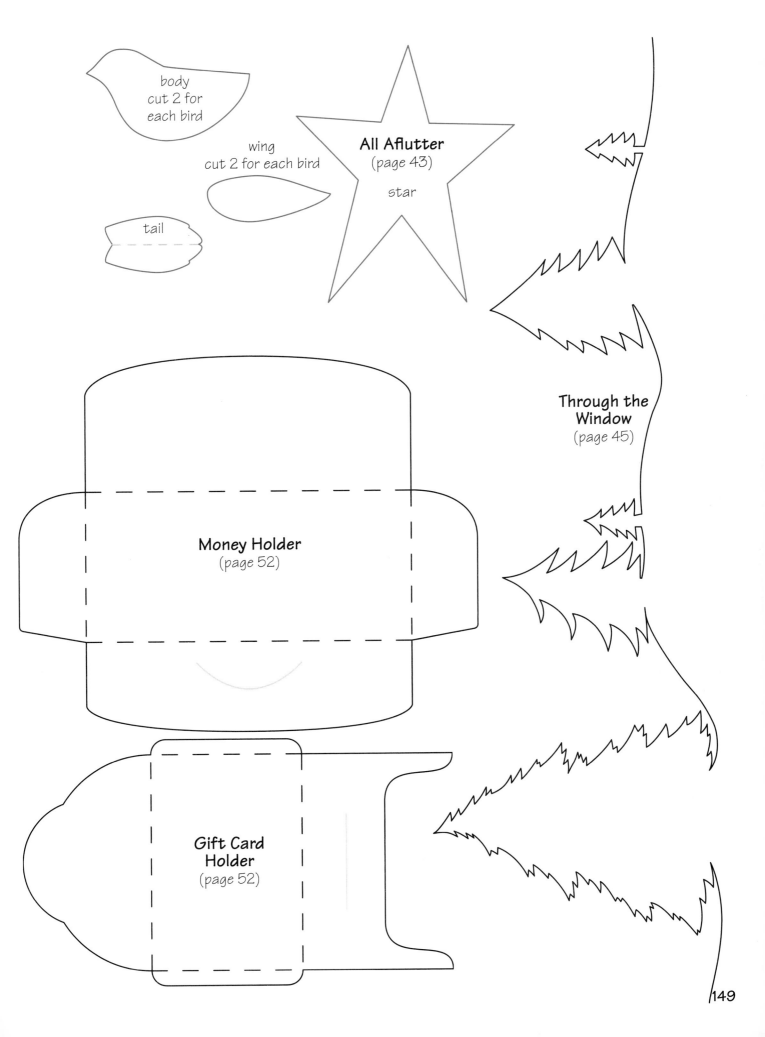

body
cut 2 for
each bird

wing
cut 2 for each bird

tail

All Aflutter
(page 43)

star

Money Holder
(page 52)

Gift Card
Holder
(page 52)

**Through the
Window**
(page 45)

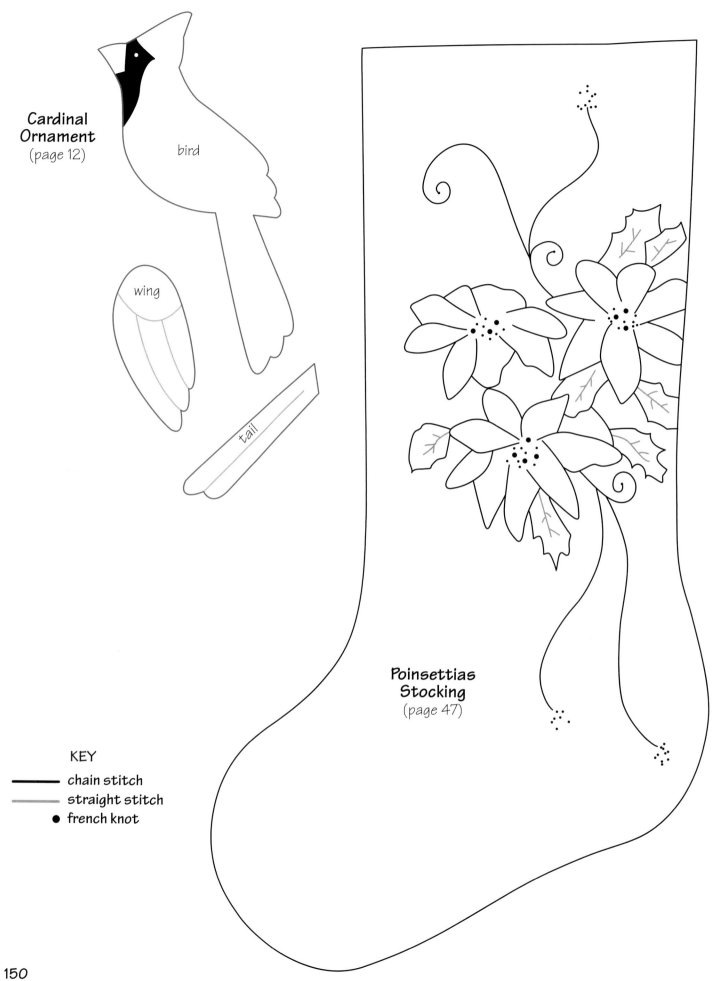

Cardinal Ornament
(page 12)

bird

wing

tail

Poinsettias Stocking
(page 47)

KEY
— chain stitch
— straight stitch
• french knot

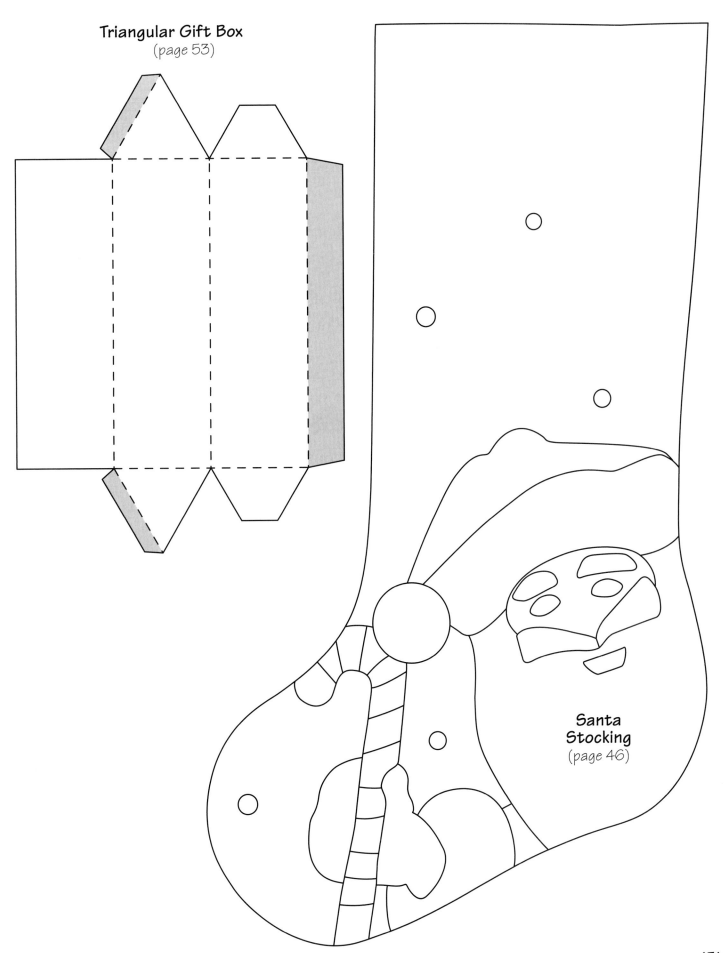

Triangular Gift Box
(page 53)

Santa Stocking
(page 46)

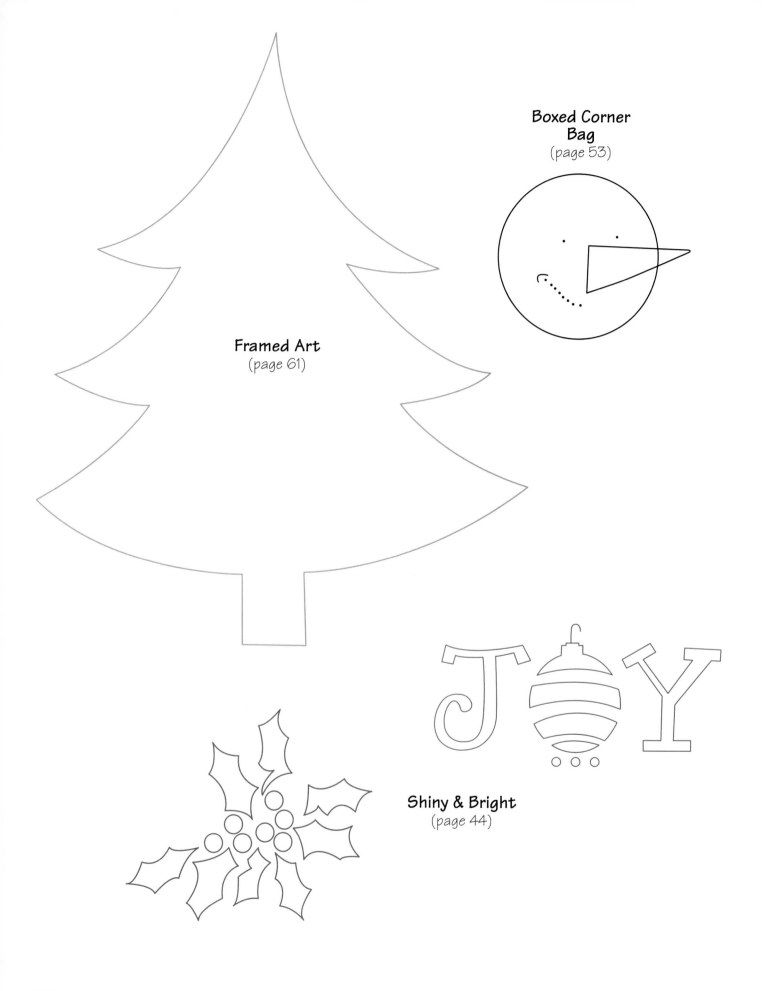

Boxed Corner
Bag
(page 53)

Framed Art
(page 61)

Shiny & Bright
(page 44)

KEY

⎯⎯ blanket stitch

⎯⎯ stem stitch

⎯⎯ straight stitch

● french knot

⎯⎯ backstitch

⎯⎯ lazy daisy stitch

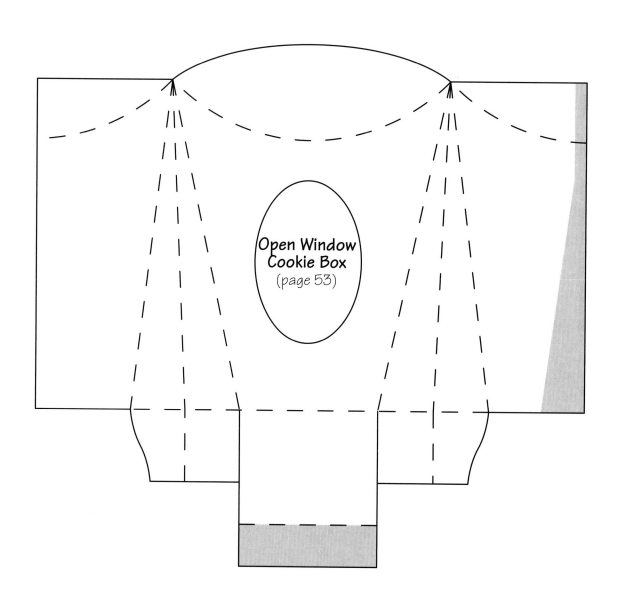

Open Window
Cookie Box
(page 53)

Tractor Hat
(page 56)

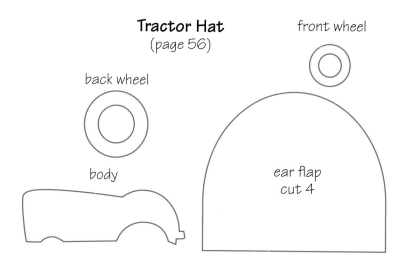

back wheel

front wheel

body

ear flap
cut 4

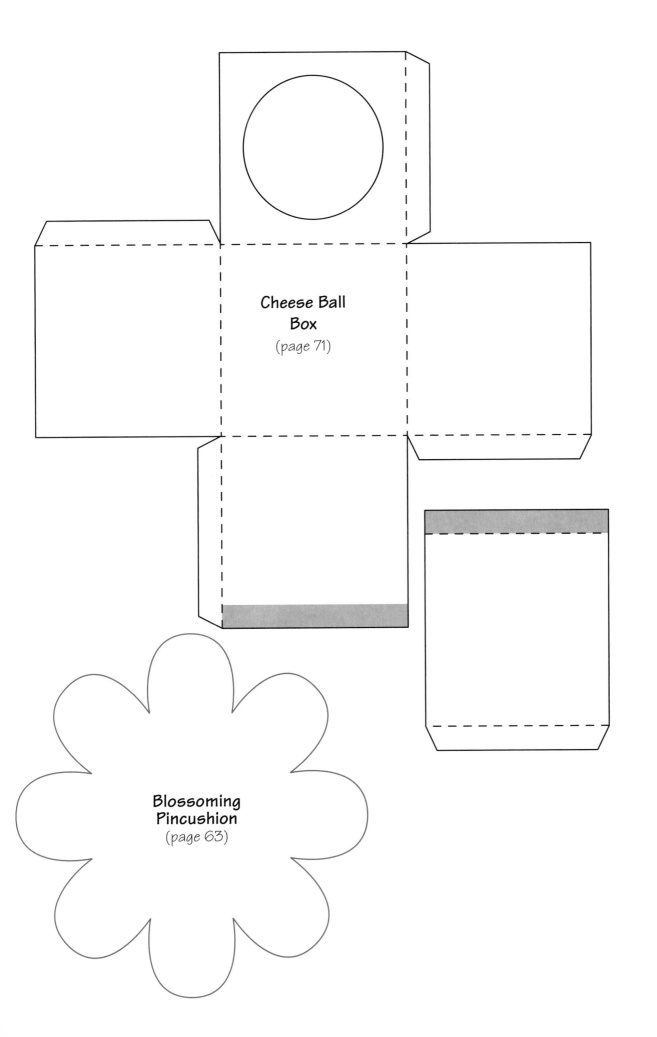

Cheese Ball
Box
(page 71)

Blossoming
Pincushion
(page 63)

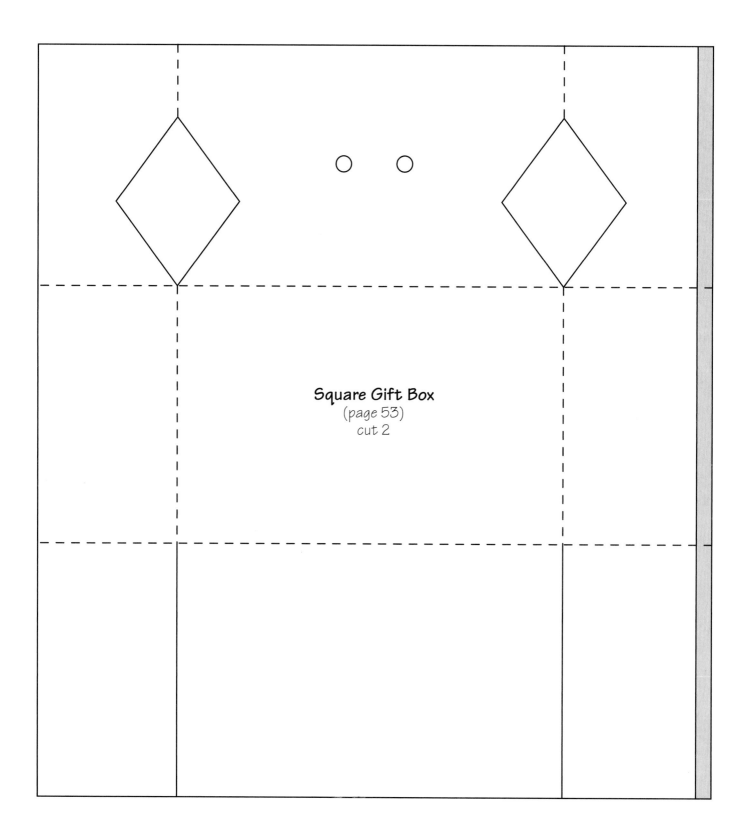

Square Gift Box
(page 53)
cut 2

Mitten Puppet
(page 56)

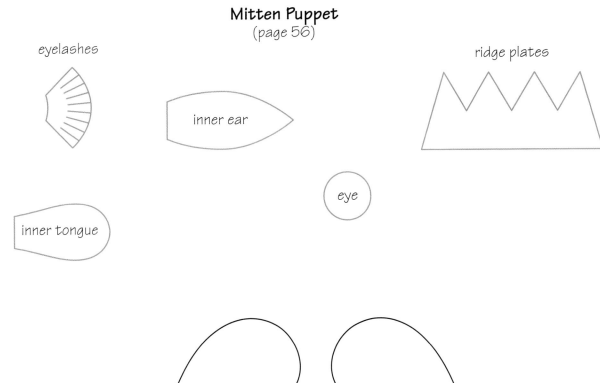

eyelashes

inner ear

ridge plates

eye

inner tongue

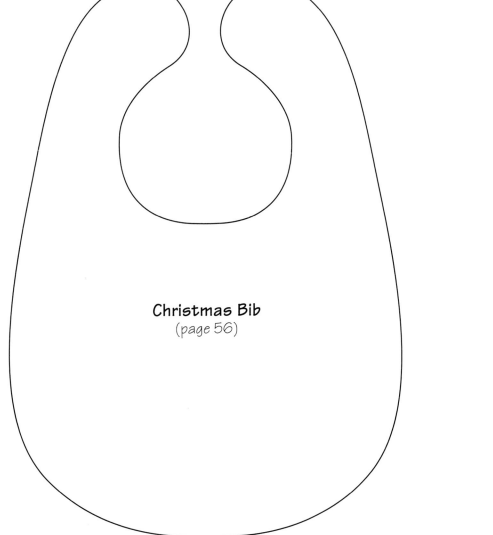

Christmas Bib
(page 56)

Project Index

Clothing & Accessories
Big, Beautiful Tote, 58
Blooming Apron, 41
Bow-Tied Apron, 64
Charming Jewelry, 59
Vintage Fabric Scarf, 57

Food Gift Packaging
Ball Ornament, 77
Cake Box, 67
Candy Glass, 73
Card, 69
Cheese Ball Box, 71
Chip & Dip Mix Container, 68
Cookie Bucket, 76
Gift Box, 71
Macaroons 4 U! Box, 68
Parfait Glass Bouquet, 74
Pie Basket, 75
Potholder, 73
Scone Cozy, 72

Gift Tags, Cards & Wrap
Box of Tags, 52
Handmade Boxes, 53
Menswear Gift Sacks, 53
Mini Gift Sacks Advent Calendar, 49
Special Cards, 52
Wrappings, 19
Wrapped Packages, 28

Gifts
Basket Liners, 41
Big, Beautiful Tote, 58
Blossoming Pincushion, 63
Bow-Tied Apron, 64
Charming Jewelry, 59
Coiled Rag Basket, 65
Cozy Cottage Night Light, 60
Cozy Thoughts Pillows, 18
Christmas Bib, 56
Farmgirl Doll, 41
Framed Button Tree, 61
Framed Pen & Ink Scene, 21
Jar Mini-scapes, 20
Sweater Throw, 10
Tractor Hat, 56
Tree Sweater Pillow, 11

Vintage Fabric Scarf, 57
Yo-Yo Sewing Kit, 62

Home Décor & Accessories
Acorn & Pinecone Centerpiece, 24
Acorn Napkin, 27
All Aflutter, 43
Basket Liners, 41
Bell Mini-Banner Ornament, 12
Burlap Holly Wreath, 51
Button Wreath, 38
Cardinal Ornament, 12
Counting the Days Advent
    Calendar, 48
Cozy Cottage Night Light, 60
Cozy Thoughts Pillows, 18
Evergreen Spray Tablecloth, 26
Felt Pinecone, 24
Felt Poinsettia Wreath, 51
Felted Wool Acorn, 24
Framed Button Tree, 61
Framed Pen & Ink Scene, 21
Hostess Towel, 65
Jar Mini-scapes, 20
Jolly Christmas Countdown Advent
    Calendar, A, 49
Mail Box Card Holder, 19
Matchbox Garland Advent
    Calendar, 48
Mini Gift Sacks Advent Calendar,
    49
Mini Pennant Swag, 40
Mistletoe Tea Towel, 25
Monogrammed Apple Wreath, 51
Shiny & Bright, 44
Snow Day Pillow, 55
Sweater Throw, 10
Through the Window, 45
Tree Sweater Pillow, 11
Vintage Angels Wreath, 51
Window Dressing Garlands, 29
Wreath, 35

Kid Stuff
Christmas Bib, 56
Farmgirl Doll, 41
Gift Cubes, 33
Horsie, 32
Mitten Puppet, 56

Piggie, 32
Snow Day Pillow, 55
Tractor Hat, 56
Turtle Tic-Tac-Toe Toss, 33

Kitchen
Acorn Napkin, 27
Blooming Apron, 41
Bow-Tied Apron, 64
Evergreen Spray Tablecloth, 26
Hostess Towel, 65
Mistletoe Tea Towel, 25

Outdoor Décor
Door Basket, 13
Lamp Post Banner, 11
Sleigh Bell Strap, 13
Sleigh with Trees, 9

Sewing Accessories
Blossoming Pincushion, 63
Yo-Yo Sewing Kit, 62

Tree Trimmings & Stockings
"Bell Jar" Ornaments, 16
Bead Garland, 34
Bell Mini-Banner Ornament, 12
Bird Stocking, 47
Blooming Tree Skirt, 38
Cardinal Ornament, 12
Felt Flower Ornament, 39
Flower Ornament/Tree Topper, 39
Fun & Games Tree, 31
Gathered Fabric Ornament, 39
Gathered Rickrack Ornament, 39
Good Cheer Garland, 21
Holiday Words Ornaments, 34
Jar Lid Ornament, 17
Personalized Tree Ornaments, 34
Poinsettias Stocking, 47
Printed Tree Skirt, 17
Printing Block Ornaments, 18
Santa Stocking, 46
Silhouette Ornament, 60
Sock Garland, 35
Star Ornaments/Tree Topper, 34
Tree Stocking, 47

Recipe Index

Appetizers & Snacks
Artichoke-Cheese Squares, 82
Baked Pita Chips, 68
Crispy Chicken Fingers, 79
Easy Sweet-and-Sour Meatballs, 80
Ham & Swiss Rolls, 80
Loaded Potato Rounds, 81
Merry Mix, A, 71
Pineapple & Nut Cheese Ball, 71
Santa's Zesty Mix, 68
Spicy Guacamole, 81
Zesty Corn Salsa, 81

Beverages
Chocolate Eggnog, 105
Holiday Wassail, 82

Breads & Rolls
Baked Texas Orange French Toast, 110
Burst-of-Lemon Muffins, 110
Cranberry Scones, 72
Old-Fashioned Yeast Rolls, 89
Popovers, 90

Cakes & Desserts
Banana-Walnut Upside Down Cake, 96
Blueberry Cream Coffee Cake, 67
Cherry Nut Cake, 70
Chocolate Fondue, 83
Double-Coconut Cake, 94
Easiest Pumpkin Cupcakes, 105
Gingerbread with Lemon Sauce, 109
Honey-Grapefruit Granita, 113
Mississippi Mud Layer Cake, 96
Norwegian Rice Pudding, 73
Raspberry Truffle Cheesecake, 93
Strawberry Cake, 95
Sweet Potato Pound Cake, 95
Tiramisu, 91
Velvety Lime Squares, 112

Candies & Confections
Chocolate Peanut Clusters, 73
Marshmallow Popcorn Balls, 77
Mint Cookies & Cream Truffle Pops, 74

Condiments, Mixes, & Sauces
Honey-Mustard Sauce, 79
Lemon-Lime Marmalade, 111
Lemon Sauce, 109
Santa's Zesty Mix, 68

Cookies & Bars
Cheesecake Cranberry Bars, 83
Cocoa-Cherry Macaroons, 68
Key Lime-White Chocolate Chippers, 113
Oatmeal Coconut Chocolate Chip Cookies, 76
Orange-Ginger Biscotti, 112
S'more Bars, 107

Entrées
Apple-Baked Pork Chops, 106
Barbeque Chicken Pizza, 106
Beef Brisket in a Bag, 106
Cheesy Baked Spaghetti, 103
Easy Chicken Enchiladas, 102
Golden Chicken Divan, 99
Lee's Trim-The-Tree Turkey Tetrazzini, 101
Momma's Shepherd Pie, 101
Roast Turkey with Sage Butter, 85
Rosemary Pork Roast with Tangerine-Cranberry Relish, 86
Sausage & Chicken Cassoulet, 100

Pies & Pastries
Maple-Pecan Pie, 91
Mock Cherry Pies, 75
Orange Meringue Pie, 111
Rustic Apple Tart, 69

Salads & Soups
Cranberry Broccoli Salad, 89
Crunchy Salad Almondine, 88
Potato-Corn Chowder, 107

Side Dishes & Casseroles
Artichoke-Cheese Squares, 82
Caramelized Brussels Sprouts, 87
Chicken & Wild Rice Casserole, 100
Cornbread Stuffing with Sage & Sausage, 87
Early-Riser Breakfast Casserole, 103
Herb Seasoned Beans, 88
Mom's Famous Macaroni & Cheese, 101
Paula's Corn Casserole, 102
Praline-Topped Butternut Squash, 88
Sweet Onion Casserole, 87

Credits

We want to extend a warm "Thank you!" to the people who allowed us to photograph some of our projects at their homes: Scott & Angela Simon, Emily & Sid Thom and Ron & Becky Werle.

We want to especially thank Mark Mathews Photography and Ken West Photography for their excellent work.

We would like to recognize the following companies for providing some of the materials and tools we used to make our projects: Clover Needlecraft, Inc. (www.clover-usa.com) for the felting needle tool & mat and The DMC Corporation for embroidery floss.

For use of the live tree on page 31, we are grateful to Arkansas Landscape of Little Rock, Arkansas.

Special thanks to Kelly Reider for assisting with the construction of some of our photo models.

A very special thank you to Betty Werle's family for the use of the vintage linens & button box, and also to Robert & Lucille Pulliam for the red sleigh.

If these cozy Christmas ideas have inspired you to look for more Gooseberry Patch® publications, find us online at www.gooseberrypatch.com and see what's new. We're on Facebook and Twitter too, so you can keep up with us even more often!